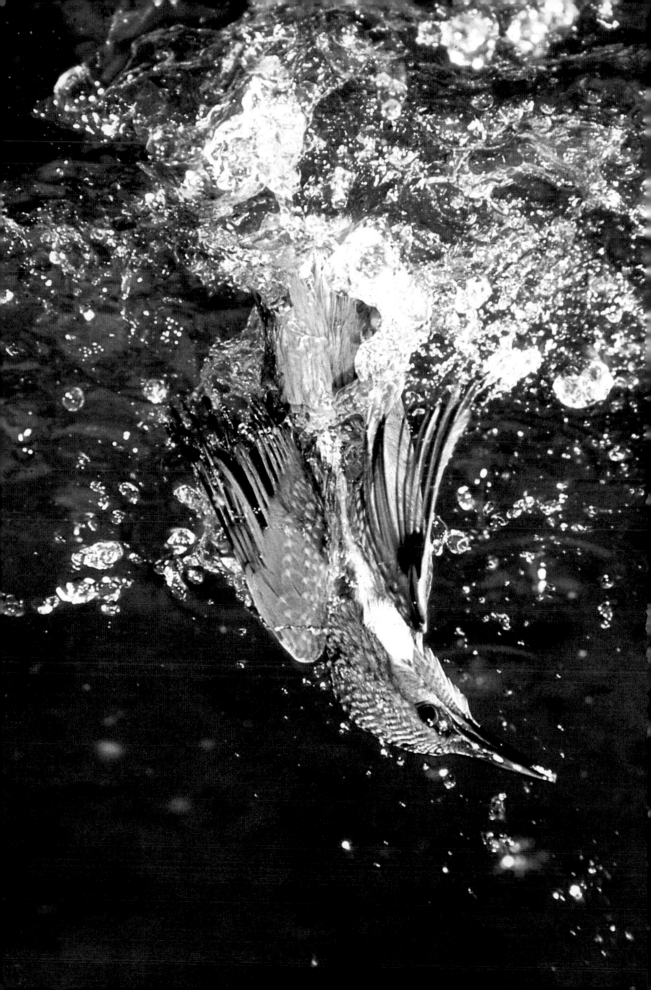

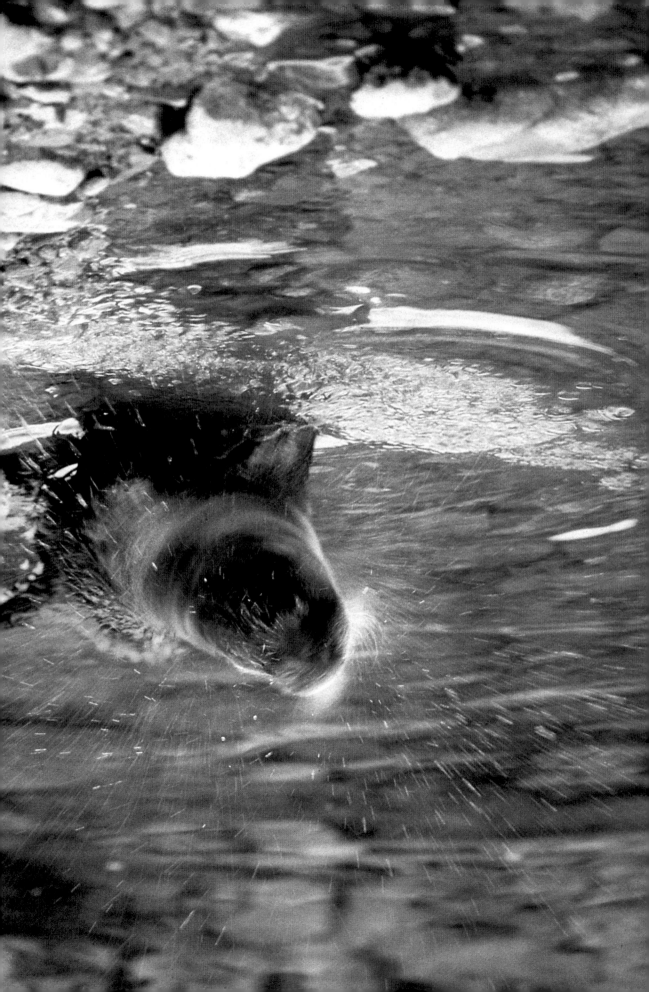

BELOVED LAND

The World of EMILY CARR

...

Introduction by Robin Laurence

Douglas & McIntyre
Vancouver/Toronto

University of Washington Press
Seattle

96 97 98 99 00   5 4 3 2 1

Douglas & McIntyre Ltd.
1615 Venables Street
Vancouver, British Columbia V5L 2H1

Canadian Cataloguing in Publication Data

Carr, Emily, 1871-1945.
        Beloved land

        ISBN 1-55054-474-8

1. Carr, Emily, 1871-1945. I. Laurence, Robin, 1950- II. Title.
ND249.C3A4 1996   759.11   C95-911185-9

Published simultaneously in the United States of America by
The University of Washington Press
PO Box 50096
Seattle, Washington 98145-5096

Editing by Saeko Usukawa
Design by George Vaitkunas
Cover painting, detail from *Big Raven* by Emily Carr, oil on canvas, 87.3 × 114.4 cm, Vancouver Art Gallery, 42.3.11
Page 3, detail from *Young Pines and Sky* c. 1935, oil on paper, 89.2 × 58.3 cm, Vancouver Art Gallery, Emily Carr Trust, 42.3.80.
Photographs of paintings and drawings by Trevor Mills, except for *Overhead* on pages 90 and 91 by Jim Jardine

Printed and bound in Hong Kong by C&C Offset Printing Co. Ltd.

The publisher gratefully acknowledges the assistance of the Canada Council and of the British Columbia Ministry of Tourism, Small Business and Culture.

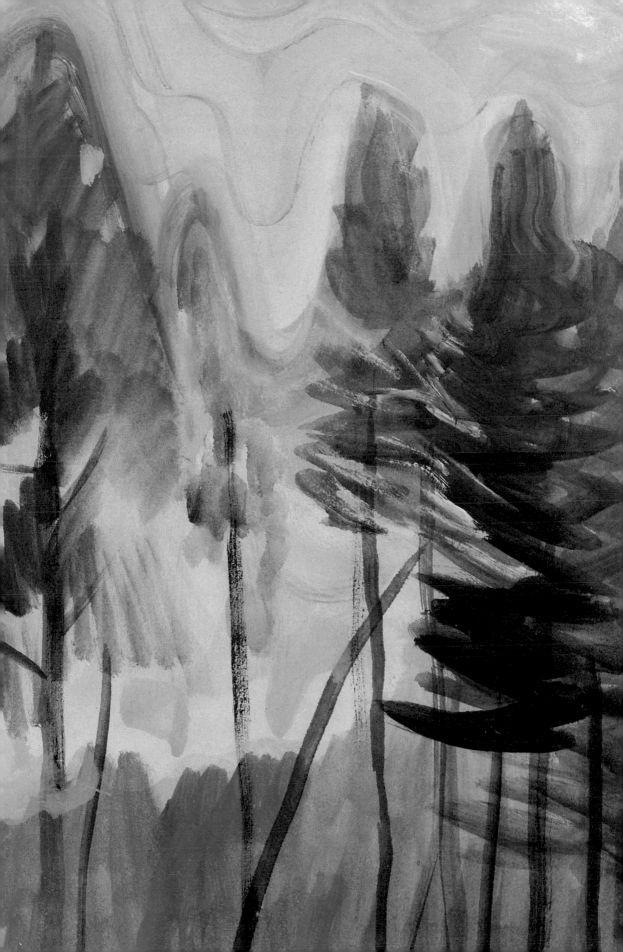

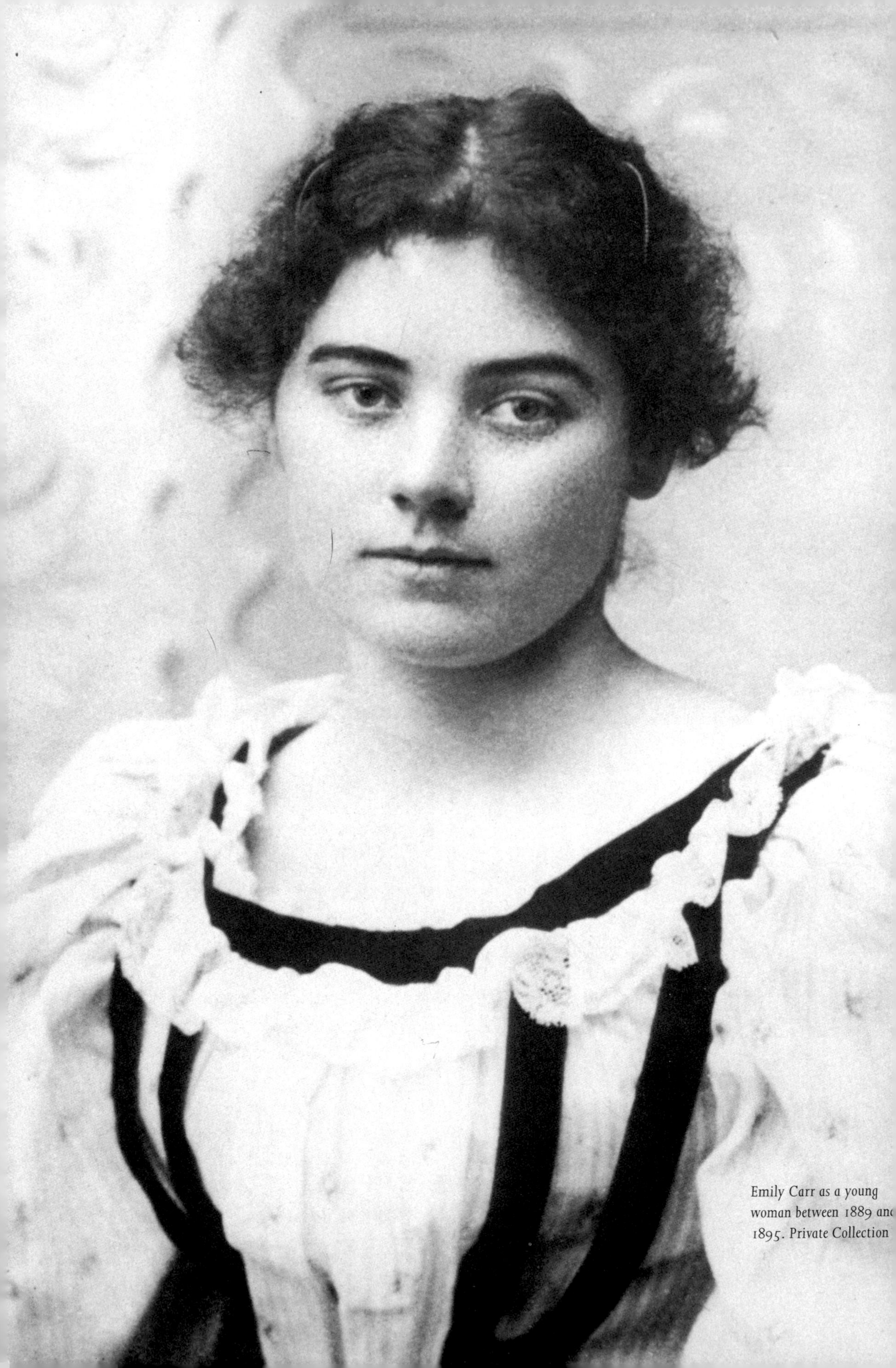

Emily Carr as a young woman between 1889 and 1895. Private Collection

EMILY CARR

by Robin Laurence

WIND WHISTLES through the trees at one end of Victoria's Ross Bay Cemetery, traffic hums by at the other. The grave of Emily Carr lies, with those of her parents, brother and sisters, close to the cemetery's north wall, identified by a simple stone marker:

EMILY CARR

1871–1945

ARTIST AND AUTHOR

LOVER OF NATURE

It is a place of gentle pilgrimage. Visitors walk among the plots and monuments and leave small offerings beside Carr's gravestone—a cluster of pine cones, a clutch of dried flowers. There is a sense of close connectedness here: Emily Carr's grave is little more than a mile from the house where she was born. The wild spots in between, the tangled woods and overgrown meadows where she played as a child, have long since disappeared, replaced by well-groomed parks, houses, lawns, and gardens. But the steep cliffs and the rocky shore below Dallas Road, the drifting seaweed and the crying sea birds and the mountains of the Olympic Peninsula across the wide, cold strait, these are as they must have been when she first knew them. The large property where she grew up—with its cow barn and pasture, vegetable garden and grapevines, fruit trees and evergreens—is now reduced to a narrow yard and a circular drive. Yet the house itself stands as it did, tall and self-confident. Here, too, visitors wander and murmur, searching through the high rooms, trying to catch some sense of a great artist, a great woman, who struggled to give form to a vision of place. The success of that struggle is evident in the extraordinary degree to which Emily Carr is identified with the Pacific coast of Canada, with the dense rain forests and monumental native carvings of the land she so fiercely loved.

■ ■ ■

THROUGH HER PAINTINGS and drawings, Emily Carr expresses much of who she was. She expresses much of herself through her writing, too, although the published stories and autobiographical sketches are not always historically accurate. Emily Carr altered the facts of her life to suit the shape of the story—and the form of her own myth. Still, the feelings and interactions are clear and true. The impression we get from Carr's remembrances—and from the remembrances of those who knew her—is of a woman spiky with contradictions. Love and anger. Determination and self-doubt. Courage and pain.

A deeply Christian person, Carr nonetheless chafed against the pieties and constraints of organized religion. She found churches "stuffy" and sought God, instead, in thick woods and forest clearings, on log-strewn beaches and under wide, sunny skies. And in her art. Painting, for her, was an act of mystical communion. It was also an act of defiance in a time and a place in which art was considered not a plausible vocation for a woman but merely a genteel diversion—like embroidery. Perhaps because of the implausibility of her life's work, Emily Carr was a determined eccentric, a notable—if conflicted—nonconformist.

Although Emily Carr scorned Victorian conventions and the opinion of its polite society, she longed for understanding and approbation—of her family, of her fellow artists, of a broader public. She was depressed and discouraged by years of negative or indifferent reception to her art, yet was suspicious of praise and success when they finally attended her. Perhaps she was too deeply invested in the notion of her aloneness, her separateness from others. Although it caused her pain, her personal and geographic isolation afforded a place for the creation of a distinctive expression of being in the world.

■ ■ ■

AS EMILY CARR TOLD IT, she was born during a December snowstorm, an apt metaphor since she raged and stormed and blew great drifts of temper through much of her life. In autobiographical sketches, she portrays herself as an active, messy and impulsive child, a black sheep in the company of her pious, neat and biddable sisters.

Almost from the beginning, she seemed to define herself in opposition to the family and society into which she had been delivered. Her middle-class, English parents, Emily and Richard Carr, had settled in Victoria, at the southern end of Vancouver Island, in 1863. Despite its veneer of "civilization," its English manners and customs, Victoria was, in its isolation, small size and rough history, an unlikely garden for the growing of a great artist. During Emily Carr's childhood, the city supported no galleries or museums where she might view historic or contemporary art, no colleges or universities where she might pursue art studies, no professional artists—and certainly no women artists—on whom she might model herself. No artists in Emily Carr's family, either, but nevertheless, she was given private drawing lessons as a young child and again as a teenager.

In the early forging of Emily Carr's psyche, however, family, religion and nature were far more important than the viewing or making of art. She was the youngest of five daughters and maintained lifelong bonds with the two sisters closest to her in age, Lizzie and Alice. Three brothers had died in infancy before Emily was born; a fourth survived childhood but died of tuberculosis at the age of twenty-three. Their mother was also frail and tubercular, a semi-invalid who died when Emily was fourteen, and about whom Emily carried a burden of guilt, believing she had pained and disappointed her. But most imposing in all the family dynamic was their father.

Richard Carr was a self-made man, a prosperous wholesaler of groceries and liquors who was characterized by his daughter Emily as the "ultra-English" and autocratic head of the family. In her early years, Emily was deeply attached to him, and he to her. She was seen as his favourite, a kind of surrogate son, and was often in his company. But she broke away from him after an obscure sexual incident in her early teens and loathed him thereafter. She professed to feel not grief but relief when Richard Carr died in 1888, two years after the death of his wife. Nonetheless, Emily's intense early identification with her father may have given her the strength to defy gender roles, to refuse marriage and motherhood in the pursuit of her art and to paint "like a man." More sinisterly, it may be that her relationship with him, whether constructed of love or loathing, made it impossible for her to connect sexually with other men. The sublimation of Emily Carr's erotic feelings into her art has been the subject of much writing and speculation, since her late landscape paintings are charged with sexual forms and energies. (She would have been horrified to read this. Unconventional as she was in many ways, Emily Carr was conventionally prudish.)

Family life was infused with Protestant morality, with daily family prayers, Bible readings, missionary meetings, church-going and Sunday school. Undoubtedly, this early and intense exposure to Christianity conditioned Emily Carr's spirituality. But beyond house, church and Sunday school existed, for her, the more sacred realm of nature. The child Emily spent as much time as possible outdoors, in the barnyard, meadow and woods, amongst the trees and animals she loved. In nature was joyous connection. Looking back on her childhood, Carr wrote about riding the family pony through the woods to "the deep lovely places that were the very foundation on which my work as a painter was to be built."

■ ■ ■

IN 1890, at the age of eighteen, Emily Carr persuaded her legal guardian to allow her to study art at the California School of Design in San Francisco. Although this move demonstrates youthful determination and commitment to her vocation, it was not exactly a bold escape from Victoria and its constraints. While away, she was supervised by a family friend and, later, by her sisters. Nor did her time in San Francisco introduce Carr to any progressive art practices: the school was conservative in its tastes and teaching methods. Carr drew from still-life arrangements and plaster casts; out of her own aversion to nudity, she refused to attend the life-drawing classes that might have enlivened her line and altered her perceptions. She achieved no creative break-throughs but merely honed the uninspired, representational style in which she had already been working.

In 1893, a downturn in her family's finances forced Carr to leave art school and return to Victoria. There she set up her first studio, converting the loft in the cow barn into a serviceable space in which she could work and give private art lessons to children. During the following years of teaching, exhibiting and saving money, she undertook an important trip to Ucluelet, a native community on the west coast of Vancouver Island. Significant during this expedition, which took place in the summer of 1898 or the spring of 1899, was her new awareness of—and attraction to—native life and culture. Growing up, the rebel in Emily Carr had envied what she saw as the freedom—of movement, dress and behaviour—that native people seemed to enjoy. At the same time, she must have observed the antipathy and scorn with which native people were treated by whites, and identified her "outsider" self with them.

Although the Nuu-chah-nulth people who lived at Ucluelet were considerably affected by disease and the social stresses of colonization and acculturation, they still preserved traditional lifeways and a closeness to the natural world that Carr deeply admired. She made a number of pencil, pen and watercolour sketches of the native villages near Ucluelet, their inhabitants, communal houses and canoes. Although she didn't—then or ever—speak any native languages, she communicated with her subjects by gestures and facial expressions, and was given the name "Klee Wyck," meaning "the laughing one."

Desperate to live independently from her family and to further her art studies, Emily Carr left Victoria for England in August 1899. She enrolled in the Westminster School of Art in London but, again, the institution was conservative and the instruction, unexceptional. Again, Carr made no real creative progress. Equally hindering to the development of her art was her reaction to London itself; she found the big, noisy, sooty city oppressive and was plagued with health problems while there. Relief was afforded by occasional trips to the countryside, and in the fall and winter of 1901-02, she lived and studied in St. Ives, Cornwall, a fishing village with an active artists' colony.

Carr took instruction in St. Ives from Julius Olsson, a minor painter of Impressionist seascapes, and his assistant, Algernon Talmage. Of the two, Carr found Talmage the more sympathetic. He understood her aversion to painting on the seashore in the brilliant sun, as Olsson wanted his students to do, and her preference for working in the "haunting, ivy-draped, solemn" Tregenna Wood above the village. Although she was years away from evolving her distinctive style, Emily Carr was beginning to discover the forest as her subject, its "indescribable depths and the glories of the greenery, the coming and going of crowded foliage that still had breath space between every leaf." Carr continued her study of trees and woods in Bushey, Hertfordshire, under the watercolourist John Whiteley. However, she returned shortly to London and there suffered a serious breakdown, both physical and emotional. In January 1903, she was admitted to a sanatorium in Suffolk, where she remained for fourteen wretched months.

Controversy and retrospective diagnoses have buzzed around Emily

Carr's illness. Some believe that her symptoms—including depression, headaches, nausea, numbness, a limp and a stutter—were the result of what was then called "hysteria" and is now called "conversion reaction," a condition in which the repression of trauma, conflict or desire is converted to physical symptoms. Others suggest that Carr was suffering from stress and discouragement over her lack of creative progress, aggravated by a series of physical ailments, an uncongenial environment, and an unhappy confrontation with the idea of marriage. Before her breakdown, Carr had been visited by William "Mayo" Paddon, a young man who had chastely courted her in Victoria. He pressed his suit in England and was rebuffed, but not without a reaction of guilt and depression in Carr. Whatever the psycho-sexual aspects of her choice not to marry, she must also have understood its political implications: marriage and art were incompatible vocations for women in her time.

After her discharge from the sanatorium, Carr returned to Bushey for a few more months of study with Whiteley, then departed for Canada in June 1904—in a mood of deep unhappiness. She was still unwell and believed herself a failure who had achieved nothing in her nearly five years abroad.

■■■

BACK HOME in Victoria, Emily Carr re-established her studio, resumed her teaching activities, and began contributing political cartoons to a local paper. However, the city was still a cultural backwater, and life in the family home was stifling under the rules and disapprovals of older sisters. When Carr was offered a teaching job in Vancouver, she took it, moving across the Strait of Georgia in January 1906.

Emily Carr lived in a boarding house in what is now downtown Vancouver, rented a studio nearby, and established herself as a successful art teacher of children. She also exhibited her own works locally— landscapes, portrait subjects and still lifes—and they were well received by both critics and public. Personally, however, she was beginning to be seen as something of an eccentric and difficult character, often at odds with her colleagues and overly attached to her "creatures"—her sheepdog Billie and assorted birds and rodents. (Throughout her life, she maintained a menagerie of beloved animals.)

Carr's closest friendship at this time was with Sophie Frank, a Salish woman who lived on a reserve in North Vancouver. Sophie Frank's life was deeply marked by tragedy: not one of the twenty-one children she

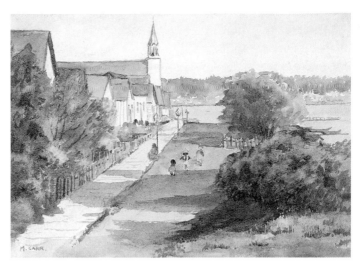

bore survived into adulthood. Childless in completely different ways, raised in completely different cultures, the two women forged a relationship that lasted some thirty years.

Emily Carr drew and painted conservative little scenes around Vancouver and at the reserve in North Vancouver. She was especially attracted to the deep forests of Vancouver's Stanley Park, applying her English watercolour training and sense of the picturesque to the stands of towering evergreens that still existed there. The results were not entirely successful. Laboured and unlimber, her Stanley Park pictures attempt to convey a sense of sanctuary in nature, but they don't begin to suggest the spiritual power and formal accomplishment Carr would achieve later.

The other important theme of Emily Carr's life and work, Northwest Coast native culture, received a great impetus in the summer of 1907, when she took a "pleasure trip" to Alaska with her sister Alice. During their travels, the two women spent a week in Sitka, on Baranof Island. There, for the first time, Emily Carr encountered the monumental sculpture—crest poles, mortuary poles, house frontal poles—of the northern Northwest Coast natives. She sketched excitedly in the native village and in an area known as "Totem Walk," where poles of the Kaigani Haida were on display for visitors.

While in Sitka, Carr met the American artist Theodore J. Richardson, who had made a successful career of incorporating native subject matter of Alaska into his own watercolours. He encouraged her and planted the tiny seed of an immense project. Emily Carr resolved to dedicate herself to depicting the great aboriginal art of British Columbia: "The Indian people and their Art touched me deeply ... By the time I reached home my mind was made up. I was going to picture totem poles in their own village settings, as complete a collection of them as I could."

It was a bold—if naive—resolution, and one that gave a profound focus to Emily Carr's art-making. Although today her work on native art themes may be seen as cultural trespass or "appropriation," or as a manifestation of an essentially paternalistic mission of "salvage," at the time it reflected a sincere desire to preserve evidence of what Carr

INDIAN RESERVE,
NORTH VANCOUVER
c. 1905
watercolour on paper
19.4 × 27.1 cm
Vancouver Art Gallery, gift
of Miss Jean McD. Russell,
81.8

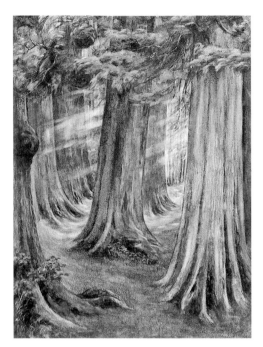

WOOD INTERIOR
1909
watercolour on paper
72.5 × 54.3 cm
Vancouver Art Gallery,
Emily Carr Trust, 42.3.86

understood to be disappearing cultural forms. By the late nineteenth century, disease, missionizing and government policy had so decimated and demoralized northern tribal groups like the Haida and Tsimshian that monumental carving had ceased. (Among the Haida, art forms and traditions continued to be passed on through the making of silver jewellery and miniature carvings in wood or a soft black stone called argillite.) The great poles produced during the "classic period" of Northwest Coast art appeared to be under threat, carried away for museums and private collectors, damaged by weather, neglect or vandalism. Those left standing in deserted villages were rotting or being consumed by the rain forest.

Over the next twenty-three years, Emily Carr made eight extended trips along the British Columbia coast and into the interior, visiting more than thirty native village sites, some occupied, some abandoned, many isolated and difficult to reach. The hundreds of drawings and watercolour sketches she made during these expeditions served as the resource for the oil paintings and more finished watercolours on native themes which she produced in her studio throughout the rest of her career. During the summers of 1908 and 1909, Carr visited Kwakiutl settlements on northern Vancouver Island, where art and ceremonial traditions had been maintained, and she was excited at the sight of vivid house frontal paintings and poles, both new and old. In the southern parts of the coast and the interior, where totem poles were not part of the material cutlure, she drew village sites, communal houses and native people. Her drawings and paintings of native subjects in these early years were conservative and fussily representational: they evince a sense of mission but lack a consolidating style or vision.

■ ■ ■

DURING BUSY YEARS teaching and exhibiting in Vancouver, Emily Carr had been saving money with the intention of studying art in Paris. In July 1910, in the company of her sister Alice, she set out for France. Even in the distant reaches of British Columbia, Carr had been hearing murmurs about the great innovations occurring in French art. With characteristic determination, she decided to learn something about it: "I wanted *now* to find out what this 'New Art' was about . . . Something in it stirred me, but I could not at first make head or tail of what it was all about. I saw at once that it made recent conservative painting look flavourless, little, unconvincing."

The "new art" Emily Carr looked for in Paris was not the radical Cubism of Picasso and Braque but a kind of "generic Post-Impressionism" that combined aspects of Impressionism, Post-Impressionism and Fauvism. These included dots, dashes or broad passages of pure or non-naturalistic colour, flattened perspective, bold patterning and painterly brush strokes. Inhibited by language, Carr sought access to French painting through Henry (Harry) Phelan Gibb, an English artist based in Paris who had been influenced by his friend Matisse. Gibb advised her to enrol in classes at the Académie Colarossi, an art school of progressive reputation. However, she felt oppressed by its all-male atmosphere and her own inability to understand the instruction and criticism given in French. She left the Colarossi to study with the Scottish-born artist John Duncan Fergusson, a colourist in the Fauve manner. His work is distinguished by simplified forms, flat passages of bright colour and a thick "reddish-purple outline," an outline that found its way into Carr's own paintings. Her instruction with him lasted only a few weeks, however, broken off by another collapse into illness.

Emily Carr was hospitalized with a combination of physical com-plaints and depression, aggravated again by her deep disaffection for big cities. She spent six weeks in a student infirmary, then travelled with Alice to Sweden, where she recovered her health. In the spring of 1911 she returned to France and joined a landscape painting class in Crécy-en-Brie, led by Harry Gibb. Emily Carr flourished in the more congenial environment of this "quaint" canal town near Paris, sketch-ing and painting *en plein air*. Although she was acutely aware that Gibb believed women artists were inferior to the male variety, she made an important creative connection with him, and followed him and his wife to St. Efflam in Brittany to continue her studies through the sum-mer. As with the native people of British Columbia, Carr was drawn to the peasants and poor country folk she met while sketching. She had an aversion to sophistication, affluence and what she called "sham"— false accommodation to social conventions, manners, niceties—and she romanticized the unaffected natures, simplicity of lifestyle and

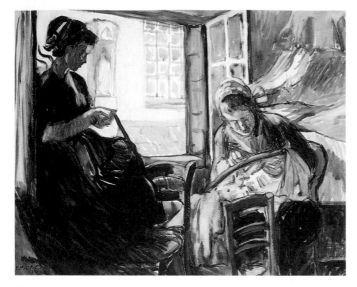

FRENCH LACE
MAKERS (WOMEN
OF BRITTANY) 1911
*watercolour and pencil on
paper*
44.5 × 54.6 cm
*Vancouver Art Gallery,
Acquisition Fund, 94.63*

generosity of those living outside the margins of middle-class Victorian society. In Crécy-en-Brie, St. Efflam, and again in Concarneau—a fishing port in Brittany where she spent her last six weeks in France, studying watercolour techniques with the expatriate New Zealand artist Frances Hodgkins—Carr often took working-class women as her subject.

Of greater consequence to her later art, however, was the landscape subject. In France, Carr's landscapes evolved through a number of experimental modes and practices, from dappled Impressionism to Fauvist scenes using bold lines, thick brush strokes, flattened perspectives and broad passages of intense colour. The ink drawings from this period are swift, rolling, beautifully reduced, and her watercolours, especially those she made while studying with Hodgkins, progressed from fussy, Anglo-Victorian images to brisk, fresh, simplified forms, richly coloured and darkly outlined. Carr's creative breakthrough was not simply one of style but of concept: she had learned an entirely new way of thinking about art. She understood now that she needn't be constrained by the literal representation of a scene, that the painting could be an autonomous entity keyed to the flatness of the picture plane and the joyful materiality of the medium. In France, Emily Carr became a modernist.

Carr sailed for home in October 1911, but not before two of her paintings had been hung in the Salon d'Automne in Paris, a huge annual exhibition of progressive and radical art. She arrived in Victoria in November, moved back to Vancouver in January, and gave an exhibition of her French paintings and watercolours in her studio in March. Although there was a large public turnout, with a mostly positive critical response, Carr later wrote that her French works were met with anger, scorn and insult. Still, she was determined to apply what she had learned in France to the landscape and indigenous culture of the West Coast. In an impassioned reply to a carping letter in a local newspaper, Carr declared, "The new ideas are big and they fit this big land."

She set off to capture that bigness. In the summer of 1912, Emily Carr undertook her most difficult and ambitious sketching trip yet. Travelling by steamship, train, stern-wheeler, canoe and fishing boat, staying in a variety of accommodations from comfortable to crude, she visited native villages and former village sites on northern Vancouver Island, on the upper reaches of the Skeena River, and on the Queen Charlotte Islands (now also known as Haida Gwaii). She made drawings and watercolours of great and collapsing stands of carved crest poles; of welcome figures, mortuary poles and house interior posts; of house frontal paintings, communal houses and war canoes. Difficulties included bad weather, stinging nettles, clouds of mosquitoes, feelings of dread and desolation amongst the abandoned poles, houses and graves, and occasional hostility and resentment from native people. Yet her watercolours of this trip, although often awkward, demonstrate a dashing brush and vivid accents of non-naturalistic colour. The oils Carr developed from her sketches make use of a somewhat flattened perspective and a more conservative, late-Impressionist palette, the paint applied with small, broken brush strokes.

A conflict is evident, however, between the ideas and techniques Emily Carr learned in France and her desire to truthfully record the poles and villages of Northwest Coast native people. The documentary impulse behind her 1907 resolution clashed with modernist self-expression, with her new longing to simplify form, juice up her brush strokes, employ heightened or non-naturalistic colour, and experiment with two-dimensional patterns. The poles and other native art works she encountered were complex and sophisticated in their features and designs. In an attempt to record their details, Carr often resorted to black outlines, evident in both her watercolours and her oils. Although this outline could be seen as a Post-Impressionist device, it does not always succeed as a formal element in her work. Instead, the evolved forms and traditions of one culture are uncomfortably overlaid with the experimental techniques of another. However, the small landscapes and city views Carr produced in Vancouver and Victoria in 1912 and 1913 demonstrate just how boldly Fauvist and forward-thinking her painting could be when applied to a non-native subject.

In April 1913, after a winter of energetic work in her studio, Emily Carr mounted an exhibition in a rented hall in Vancouver. She displayed more than two hundred of her native-inspired paintings, drawings and watercolours, created over a period of fourteen years, and she also lectured to the public twice during the show's week-long run. Carr spoke about native people and culture and her own experiences among them, extolling their honesty, dignity and creative genius.

Although now she could be criticized for a benign racism that generalized and romanticized native people and culture, she also could be admired for lobbing her positive observations at the stony wall of social and cultural prejudice, for arguing against the negative stereotypes about natives that existed in the minds of her white audience. Emily Carr also promoted the great accomplishments of native artists as a valuable part of Canadian cultural heritage.

Although the exhibition was well reviewed in the local press, sales were poor, and Carr had the sense that her work was being "rejected" by the public. Certainly, she was battling against not only a reactionary response to her avant-garde art but also a dismissive way of thinking about native culture. Following this show, Emily Carr entered a period of deep discouragement. Her teaching contracts had not been renewed, sales of her art had fallen off, and a bid to sell all her works on native themes to the provincial government had also failed.

■■■

SINCE SHE COULD NOT earn a living in Vancouver, Carr formed a plan: to build a small apartment building on land she had inherited from her father's estate in Victoria. She designed a suite and studio for herself in the building, and intended to support her art-making from the rent revenues. In June 1913, Emily Carr returned permanently to Victoria, but her well-laid plan was thwarted by the times. War broke out, the demand for rental housing fell, and her low rents barely covered her expenses. She could not afford to hire help and spent all her time labouring as a manager, caretaker, cook and cleaner. To supplement her meagre income over the next fifteen years, she raised purebred dogs, sold fruit, rabbits and chickens, drew cartoons for a short-lived feminist publication, painted ballroom decorations, hooked rugs, and made pottery. She incorporated native designs into her rugs and her ceramics, but felt guilty about "prostituting Indian Art," removing it from its original context and reducing it to mere decoration.

The years 1913 to 1928 were a period of great frustration and resentment for Emily Carr. Always rebellious and nonconforming, she was now obliged to put aside her waywardness and her creative aspirations and spend her time as a domestic and janitorial drudge. A dreadful paradox exists here: a woman artist who refused marriage but was later trapped by an equally stifling form of domesticity. She later wrote: "I never painted now—had neither time nor wanting. For about fifteen years I did not paint." Perhaps this is what it felt like in retrospect, but, from time to time, Emily Carr was able to paint, to sketch in nearby Beacon Hill Park, to visit her friend Sophie Frank in North Vancouver, and sometimes to take longer expeditions to spots outside Victoria. She did, indeed, relinquish the native subject in her art for some fifteen years and instead painted small, Fauvist landscapes, very much in the manner she'd learned in France. Occasionally, too, she exhibited her work, taking part in group shows in Victoria and Seattle.

Emily Carr's reputation as a crank and an isolated eccentric grew, but her work attracted the interest of a few people who understood the injustice of her lapse into discouragement and obscurity. Among her friends and supporters were the physician and amateur ethnologist Dr. Charles Newcombe and his son Willie, who together amassed an important collection of Carr's paintings and drawings. Also drawn to Carr's art and plight were the Vancouver mining executive and art patron Harold Mortimer Lamb; anthropologists Marius Barbeau and Erna Gunther; and three young Seattle artists, Viola and Ambrose Patterson and Mark Tobey. In the early 1920s, the Pattersons and Tobey encouraged Carr to spend more time painting and to actively exhibit her work again.

Eventually, Emily Carr's name came to the attention of Eric Brown, director of the National Gallery in Ottawa. He and Barbeau were jointly curating "Canadian West Coast Art, Native and Modern," an exhibition of art by Northwest Coast natives and by contemporary, non-native artists on Northwest Coast native themes. In September 1927, Brown visited Carr in her studio and selected some sixty of her paintings and watercolours, as well as rugs and pots, for possible inclusion in the show. He also recommended that she read Frederick B. Housser's *A Canadian Art Movement*, describing and championing the Group of Seven— artists of whom she then had no knowledge. On November 6, 1927, Housser's book in hand, Emily Carr set off for Toronto and Ottawa on the most momentous journey of her life.

■ ■ ■

THE EXHIBITION, which opened at the National Gallery in Ottawa and travelled to Toronto and Montreal, was a success, and Carr's work was singled out for particular praise. She was greatly cheered by the response of critics and colleagues, by her inclusion in the show along with other artists of stature, and by the wider interest that her art now generated. But she also understood her success had more to do with the native subject matter than her accomplishment as a modernist painter. More exciting for her, and far more pivotal to her development as an artist, were her meetings in Toronto with members of the Group of Seven.

Carr had read Housser's book on the train ride east and been greatly affected by it. But connecting with Group members in their studios, viewing their work and discussing it with them, had an even more extraordinary impact on her career. Formed in 1920, based in Toronto, the Group of Seven represented the most radical approach to painting in English Canada of that time. Integral to their nationalist mission of creating a truly Canadian art had been a desire to develop a style and subject matter free of Old World conventions and conservatism. That desire had resulted in the synthesis of a number of influences, including Art Nouveau and Scandinavian Post-Impressionism, applied to the landscape of the Canadian wilderness. It's ironic that the Group's declared "Canadian" style was principally European in origin; nevertheless, the Group's way of treating landscape was enormously innovative in the narrow, colonial context in which it was applied, and its members eventually became the most influential landscape painters in Canada. Through their expressed aims—including union with nature and a mystical identification with place, influenced by the American Transcendentalists—Carr was able to find a direction for her own inchoate aspirations. Through the Group's methods of handling painted form, its "boldness of patterning and colouration," she was able to conceive and evolve her own style. Too, the Group welcomed Carr warmly and provided her with a sense of community, a feeling of creative companionship after so many years of loneliness and misunderstanding.

Carr's sketching expeditions to isolated areas of British Columbia and her struggle to find a visual language for the "big land" of the West Coast accorded with the Group's mandate to find one for the northern Ontario wilderness. In her nearly fifteen-year retreat from the art world, however, Carr had fallen behind them, in both theory and technique. Contact with the Group—and especially with Lawren Harris, their unofficial leader—inspired her to resume painting in a newly focussed and energized way. Although she admired the work of other Group members, Emily Carr's connection with Harris's paintings was singular and profound. After her first visit to Harris's studio, she wrote in her journal, "Oh God, what have I seen? Where have I been?

Something has spoken to the very soul of me, wonderful, mighty, not of this world. Chords way down have been touched."

Although fourteen years Carr's junior, Harris became her most important mentor: he advised her on technical questions, encouraged her through periods of depression and self-doubt and, more significantly, helped her shape her own understanding of the spiritual in art. It was the spiritual element in Harris's austere and reductive landscapes that first called out to Carr. "I think perhaps I shall find God here," she wrote in her journal, "the God I've longed and hunted for and failed to find."

Central to Harris's art practice was his belief in Theosophy: he sought to paint landscapes (and later abstractions) imbued with a universal spirit. Carr, too, attempted to make spiritual and creative sense of Theosophical doctrines, but after some six years of struggle with its teachings, she concluded that Theosophy was not compatible with her "long-established Christian beliefs." In the meantime, however, she absorbed Harris's beliefs about the visionary role of the artist and the higher moral purpose of art.

Within a few weeks of her return to Victoria, Emily Carr had thrown herself back into her painting. "Sketch-sack on shoulder, dog at heel, I went into the woods singing," she later wrote. "Not far and only for short whiles . . . but household tasks shrivelled as the importance of my painting swelled." The success of her 1912-13 paintings in the "West Coast Art" exhibition must have stimulated her desire to return to native themes. During the winter and spring of 1928, Carr painted canvases from her earlier drawings and watercolours, and that summer—at the age of fifty-six—she undertook another long and arduous sketching expedition. For six weeks, in often difficult and sometimes dangerous conditions, she travelled to northern Vancouver Island, the Skeena and Nass river valleys, and the Queen Charlotte Islands.

The poles Emily Carr encountered, especially in the Haida and Gitksan areas, had deteriorated considerably since her last visit, some sixteen years earlier. Many had rotted, fallen and been been swallowed up by forest, or had disappeared into museum collections. In 1928, Carr ceased to include groups of native people in her depictions of monumental art, and was drawn instead to deserted villages, surrounded by loneliness and dense growth. Not only were these deserted sites free of troubling signs of acculturation, but they afforded Carr a romantic identification with place and, again, reinforced her sense of native culture as endangered.

In her new, Group-influenced approach to painting, Emily Carr employed monumental native art as both a vehicle for Canadian nationalism—evidence of an ancient culture entirely original to the New World, without any ties to Europe and therefore symbolic of this great land—and a metaphor of the artist's vocation. She had long before identified herself with the "otherness" of native peoples, and now she conflated the supposed intentions of native carvers with her own feelings for nature and her own striving after self-expression. As in her earlier paintings, however, her strong respect for the achievements of native artists competed with the formal and expressive problems with which she was grappling on the picture plane.

The style Carr evolved during the period 1928-31 was much less painterly and much more sculptural than the Post-Impressionist techniques she had employed following her studies in France. In her use of smoothly modelled, volumetric forms, subdued or sombre palette, and a kind of streamlined elimination of detail, Carr evinced the clear influence of Harris. Other similarities to his paintings included the symbolic use of light—especially slanting shafts of light—to suggest a spiritual presence, and a highly designed and geometric treatment of natural forms.

Although Carr was striving to make art that would have as powerful an emotional impact on others as Harris's paintings had on her, she learned the technical means to achieve this end from another artist, the American Mark Tobey. Carr had first met Tobey in the early 1920s, and she connected with him again in September 1928, when he came to her Victoria studio to give a three-week master class in painting. Tobey, although nineteen years younger than Carr, was responsible for giving her the tools to achieve her new vision. These tools, derived from his own recent studies in France and his enthusiastic immersion in Analytic Cubism, included a facetting of the three-dimensional forms depicted and the backlighting of objects to create dramatic effects of brightness and darkness and to articulate form. It is a curious paradox that Carr applied the "structuring" lessons of Cubism to her images of the tribal art of the Northwest Coast, since the tribal art of Africa and the South Pacific had greatly influenced the development of Cubism in France. Despite her years of looking at and depicting native art, Emily Carr seems not to have learned its strategies of stylization and spatial organization directly; rather, she learned similar techniques indirectly, through non-native artists working in the Cubist mode.

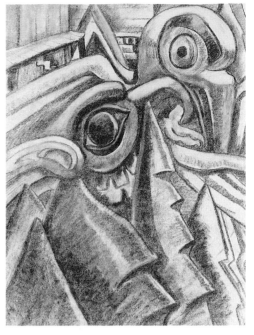

Other influences of the time were more meta-physical than technical: Carr had become a great admirer of the poetry of Walt Whitman, and it conditioned her evolving, pantheistic "view of the world." She also renewed her efforts to travel and look at art beyond parochial little Victoria, visiting Toronto and New York in 1930, and Toronto and Chicago in 1933. In New York, she saw avant-garde art of Europe and America, including Marcel Duchamp's controversial *Nude Descending a Staircase*, and briefly met Georgia O'Keeffe, whose erotic landscapes and sexualized natural forms resembled those that Carr was unconsciously and quite separately developing.

The years 1928 to 1931 are remarkable in Emily Carr's career, being a time in which she fully revived and transformed her art practice, sketched and painted prolifically, and created many of the images that are most associated with her in the public mind. Although these works manifest the influences of her mentors in form, structure and paint handling, they are also assertive of Carr's own connection with place. Over the course of these years, at the urging of Harris and Tobey, Carr relinquished the native subject and devoted herself to the landscape, but not before establishing a relationship between them—between totem and forest.

In Carr's early sketches and watercolours of native villages, the forest is merely a background element, a dark curtain behind the buildings and people that were her focus. In her French-influenced works of 1912-13, trees, bushes and high grasses are decorative components of the Post-Impressionist landscape, deployed in stippled or sinuous patterns around the native houses, people and poles, and often opening up to passages of bright sky. By 1930, however, the forest has become a more fearful and more forceful presence. Weighty and deeply sculpted, it has begun to press in on the native carvings, which are no longer depicted in groups but as isolated poles or figures, often in close-up.

As Carr wrote in *Klee Wyck*, she was sometimes unsettled by the abandoned village sites she visited, haunted as they were with tragic histories of epidemics and death, surrounded by "smothering darkness," overrun by thick tangles of second growth. In her dark, formalist works of 1929-31, Carr seems to bring her own culture's fear of the forest—European fairy tales of ogres, wolves and witches, of children lost in the woods—to her encounters with native art and myth, especially with depictions of Dzunuk̲wa, the "wild woman of the woods."

By Carr's reading, native culture emerges from and then is reclaimed by the rain forest. In some works, a balance is struck between the brilliant assertions of the native carvings and the more sombre claims of the surrounding trees. In others, the forest overwhelms. Carr conveys the frailty and ephemerality of human endeavour against the relentless and voracious power of the dark woods and the spirits that dwell there. In many paintings of this period, the sky is crowded out altogether and the great weight of the forest can be seen as symbolic not of nature but of the masculine systems of art-making and metaphysical thinking that Carr was trying to incorporate into her art.

Emily Carr's final sketching expeditions to native sites, in 1929 and 1930, took her to the west and north coasts of Vancouver Island. Although her motivation was again the recording of native culture there, she spent considerable time drawing in the forest. She was apparently responding to Harris's admonition that "the totem is a work of art in its own right" and that she should find her own symbolic equivalent in the "exotic landscape" of the West Coast.

As Carr shifted subject matter, she also shifted painting technique: tree forms are less stiff and faceted, more softened and sinuous; thick slabs of foliage give way to green draperies with parallel and concentric folds, or to swelling and swirling matter with rounded or scalloped edges. There is a new and sustained interest in movement and the rhythmic interlocking of forms, and a new—though probably unconscious— sexualizing of the forest in a drama of tumescence and regeneration. Oppositions are created in masculine, upthrusting tree trunks and feminine, downbearing foliage, with glimmers throughout of thin, cold light. The impact of Theosophy and Transcendentalism is manifest in works that express the divine spirit in all things—and the endless cycle of nature. Trees are anthropomorphized into beings, young and extroverted or old and reserved, and the forest itself opens up, dark interiors giving way to unexpected clearings and bright patches of new growth.

Having relinquished the native theme of her painting, Emily Carr no longer made long expeditions to remote village sites. Instead, she drew and painted from the landscape much closer to Victoria, frequently within walking distance of her home, in Beacon Hill Park and on the cliffs and beaches along Dallas Road. Her subjects ranged from deep woods to logged-off clearings, from gravel pits to log-strewn seashores,

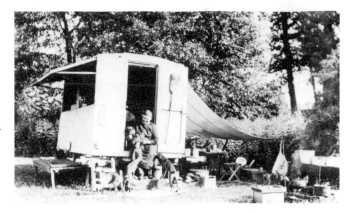

Emily Carr and her caravan, with some of her many pets, 1934. B.C. Archives and Records Service IIP65557

from energetic new growth to arching expanses of sea and sky. After 1931, Carr established a "pattern" for her sketching trips, taking one in the spring and one in the late summer or fall, with dedicated periods of painting in her studio in between. Although she maintained her apartment house until 1936, she was not now so tyrannized by it. Her financial situation had eased slightly in the 1920s and her new commitment to art directed her to make time for her true vocation.

A number of factors impelled Emily Carr through the expansive painting style of her seventh decade, including the acquisition of a caravan she named "the Elephant." She bought the squat metal van in the summer of 1933, had it fitted out to accommodate herself, her pets and her drawing materials, and then had it hauled to her chosen sketching spots. Where previously she had stayed in rented rooms and cottages, she could now enjoy a sense of independence and self-sufficiency—and could feel utterly surrounded by the natural world. Another element in Emily Carr's late liberation was her discovery of a fast-drying, versatile and economical sketching medium: artist's oil paints, thinned with gasoline, mixed with white housepaint, and applied to cheap manila paper. Throughout Carr's career, there prevails the sense that her images are hard-won. She did not possess a graceful facility of drawn line, nor a deft watercolour technique. (Many of her earlier pen, pencil and watercolour sketches are awkward and overworked, although her later charcoal drawings are handsome and well-constructed.) Yet in the oil-on-paper works created between 1933 and 1936, she achieved a tremendous fluidity and ease, an unprecedented spontaneity and expressiveness.

Their lightness, brightness and expansiveness correspond with a period in which Carr severed her ties with her male mentors, thus freeing herself to evolve her own true expression. Although she was notorious for her bad temper and her abrupt, angry ending of relationships, she established some warm friendships in Victoria, enjoyed growing recognition through local, national and international exhibitions and—most importantly—realized in art her mystical feeling of union with God and nature through the agency of landscape. In her journals, Carr advises herself, when sketching, to "sit quietly and silently acknowledge your divinity and oneness with the creator of all things." Both the oil paintings on paper and the canvases she worked up from them reveal a complete transformation from the oppressive weight and darkness of her work a few years earlier. Carr was now making a joyous—almost ecstatic—identification with the landscape, communicated in her paintings through sweeping and swirling movement, expressive brush strokes and shimmering light. Although she was still creating images of the forest interior, she was becoming more interested in open spaces and luminous skies: curiously, the gravel pits and deforested tracts of land become scenes of regeneration and religious communion. There is an emotionally charged empathy with the tall, spindly trees that have been rejected by loggers and with the jagged stumps (which she called "screamers") left in the desolate wake of logging. But even the desolation becomes transcendent with radiant skies and undulating new growth, realized with rushing, concentric brush strokes. In the late landscapes, technique is totally married to expression, formal elements to feelings of spiritual affirmation.

■■■

THE PAINTINGS and oil-on-paper works of the mid-1930s are the climax of Emily Carr's career. Changes, of course, continued to occur in her life. In early 1936, she gave up her apartment house, moved into a rented cottage, and set up her studio there. That year, she took two sketching expeditions in her caravan, and the following January, she suffered the first of three heart attacks. Over the next eight years, Carr was repeatedly hospitalized and had to contend with strokes, thrombosis and cardiac asthma, as well as other heart disease and the painful infirmities of old age. Nevertheless, she pursued her painting when she could and, although she sold the Elephant in the summer of 1938, managed to undertake a number of sketching trips. In October 1939 she had a triumphant solo show at the Vancouver Art Gallery, from which she derived the happy sense that her art had truly spoken to the people of British Columbia.

Apart from her ill health, Emily Carr's last decade is marked by her return to the native subject in her painting and her emergence as a professional writer. Carr had been a "compulsive" scribbler of prose scraps and doggerel verse since childhood. She began her serious journals, however, in 1927, on her life-changing journey to eastern Canada, and maintained them quite steadily through the years 1930 to 1941. Published in edited form after her death as Hundreds and Thousands, the journals are a spontaneous expression of her reawakening to painting, her soaring convictions and sad self-doubts, her relationships with friends, family, animals and nature, her losses and griefs, and her striving to find the art and the religion that most truly accord with her being.

Emily Carr had also begun to write short fiction and autobiographical sketches in the 1920s. She took a correspondence course in the short story in 1926, enrolled in two local courses in 1934, and began showing her stories to family and friends and sending them out to magazines (they were all rejected). She was much supported by her friend Flora Burns, who took writing courses with her and typed and copy-edited her manuscripts. Later, Carr's writing was championed by Ruth Humphrey, an English teacher at Victoria College, and later still by Ira Dilworth, regional director of radio for the Canadian Broadcasting Corporation in Vancouver. Dilworth became a close friend and confidant of Carr's last years; he also promoted her stories, arranged for their publication, and acted as her editor and literary executor.

During the months of convalescence after her 1937 heart attack, Emily Carr began concertedly to write—to complete and revise her stories and prose sketches of her encounters with native people, life and culture. The seventeen stories she composed then on native themes formed the bulk of her first published book, Klee Wyck. Between 1937 and 1941, Carr also completed the stories that would become, in published form, The Book of Small, The House of All Sorts, Growing Pains, Pause: A Sketchbook, and The Heart of a Peacock. One of the great ironies of Carr's career is that, in her lifetime, she enjoyed much greater popular success with her writing than with her painting. Klee Wyck, published in 1941, became a national bestseller and won a Governor General's Award, Canada's most prestigious literary prize. The Book of Small, recollections of her contrary childhood, was published in 1942 and also sold well, helping to make her name "a household word in Canada."

While writing and revising her native stories, Emily Carr was stirred to return to the native subject in her paintings. In some cases, she worked from old sketches and watercolours; in others, she revisited the forms of earlier oil paintings, with less forcefulness, perhaps, but with a greater serenity. The poles are no longer in danger of being swept away by a sea of undergrowth or consumed by ravenous forest; instead, tree and carved forms co-exist within a gentle swell of green foliage and silvery light. It's as if, facing death, Carr were enacting a great acceptance, a great reconciliation on her canvases. The heart of the forest is addressed too, but again with more serenity than fear. If cougars, witches and wild women still inhabit these places, Emily Carr is no longer fearful of them. Perhaps she recognizes her affinity with them.

Despite being weakened by strokes and heart attacks, Carr continued to prepare books for publication and paintings for exhibition. Her first show in a commercial gallery took place in October 1944, in the prestigious Dominion Gallery in Montreal. It was an unexpected triumph and realized a degree of financial success she had never before experienced. That success, however, came late. In February 1945, Emily Carr checked herself into a nursing home near the old family property, and on March 2, 1945, she died there.

· · ·

ALTHOUGH EMILY CARR was never politically active, never a declared feminist, she did struggle against the prevailing view that women couldn't be artists in the full sense that men could. Despite the encouragement of the Group of Seven, Carr understood soon after meeting them that, being a woman and a Westerner, she would always be an outsider in their view. Her journals of 1937 record a late resolution in her career: "I have been thinking that I am a shirker. I have dodged publicity, hated write-ups and all that splutter . . . I have been forgetting Canada and forgetting women painters. It's them I ought to be upholding." She cites a positive review of her art and continues, "I am . . . glad that I am showing these men that women can hold up their end. The men resent a woman getting any honour in what they consider is essentially their field. Men painters mostly despise women painters. So I have decided to stop squirming, to throw any honour in with Canada and women." And that is exactly what she did.

BELOVED LAND

You must be absolutely honest and true in the depicting of a totem for meaning is attached to every line. You must be most particular about detail and proportion ... Every pole in my collection has been studied from its own actual reality, in its own original setting, and I have, as you might term it, been personally acquainted with every pole.

—Emily Carr, notebook, 1913 (quoted by Kerry Mason Dodd in
SUNLIGHT IN THE SHADOWS, unpaginated)

SKIDEGATE 1912
oil on card
63.4 × 30.0 cm
Vancouver Art Gallery,
Emily Carr Trust,
42.3.73

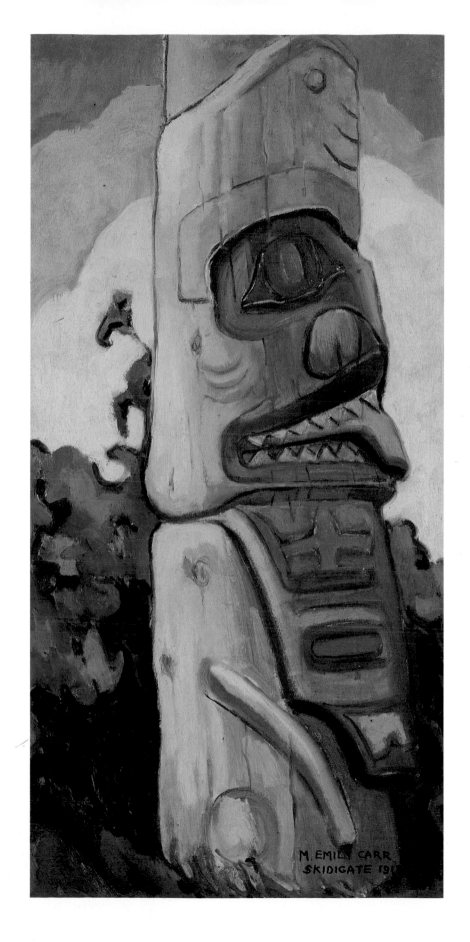

We passed many Indian villages on our way down the coast. The Indian people and their Art touched me deeply . . . By the time I reached home my mind was made up. I was going to picture totem poles in their own village settings, as complete a collection of them as I could.

—Emily Carr, GROWING PAINS (THE EMILY CARR OMNIBUS, p. 427)

TOTEM POLES,
KITSEUKLA 1912
oil on canvas
126.8 × 98.4 cm
Vancouver Art Gallery,
Founders Fund, 37.2

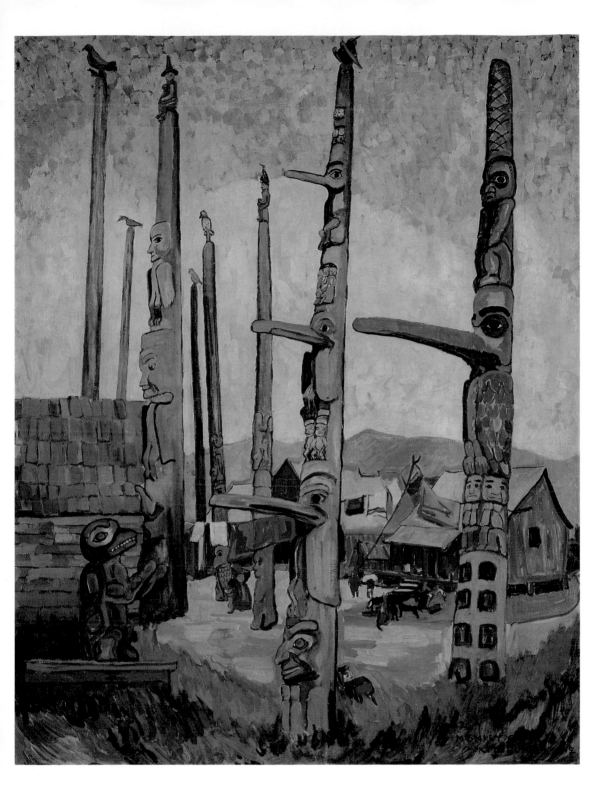

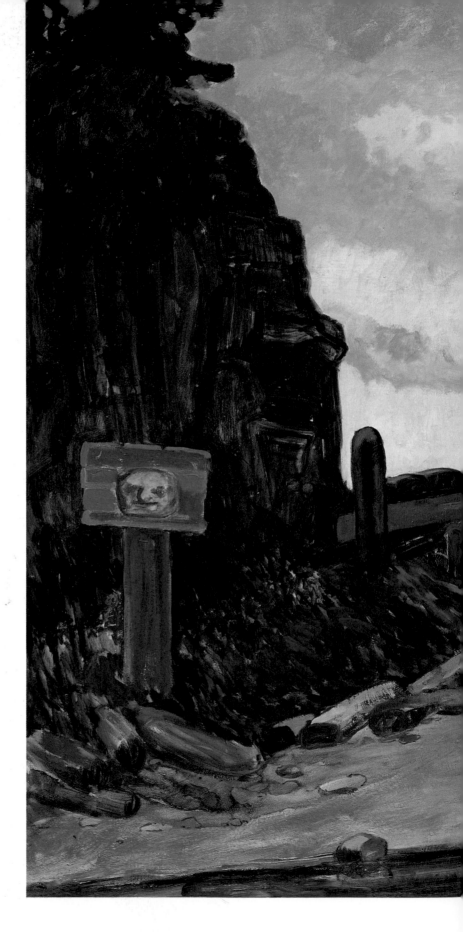

TOTEM BY THE
GHOST ROCK 1912
oil on canvas
90.2 × 114.7 cm
Vancouver Art Gallery,
Emily Carr Trust,
42.3.10

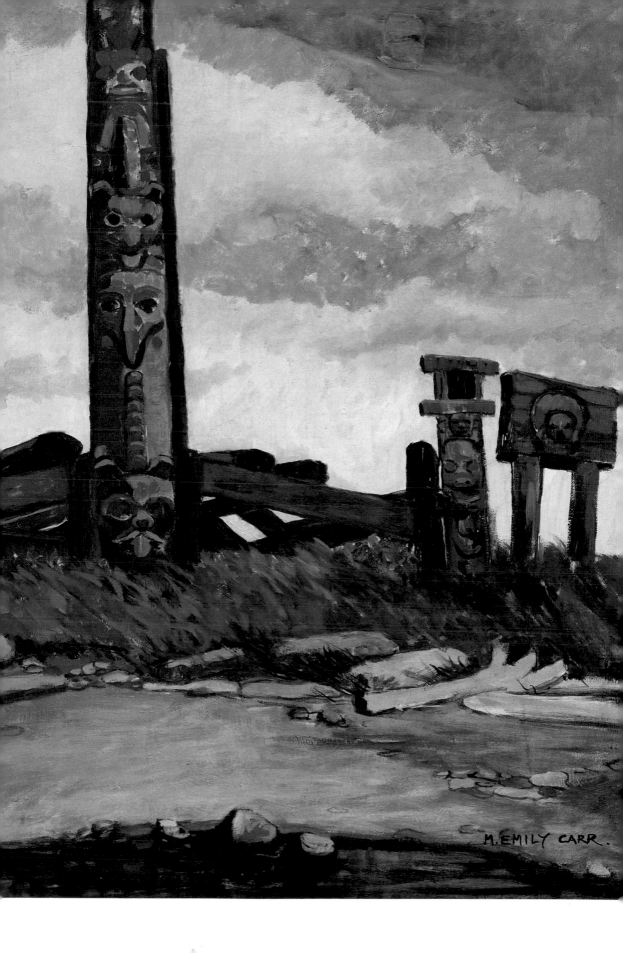

M. EMILY CARR.

The brave old totems stood solemnly round the bay. Behind them were the old houses of Yan, and behind that again was the forest . . .

Nobody lived in Yan. Yan's people had moved to the newer village of Masset, where there was a store, an Indian agent and a church.

Sometimes Indians came over to Yan to cultivate a few patches of garden. When they went away again the stare in the empty hollows of the totem eyes followed them across the sea.

—Emily Carr, KLEE WYCK (THE EMILY CARR OMNIBUS, p. 56)

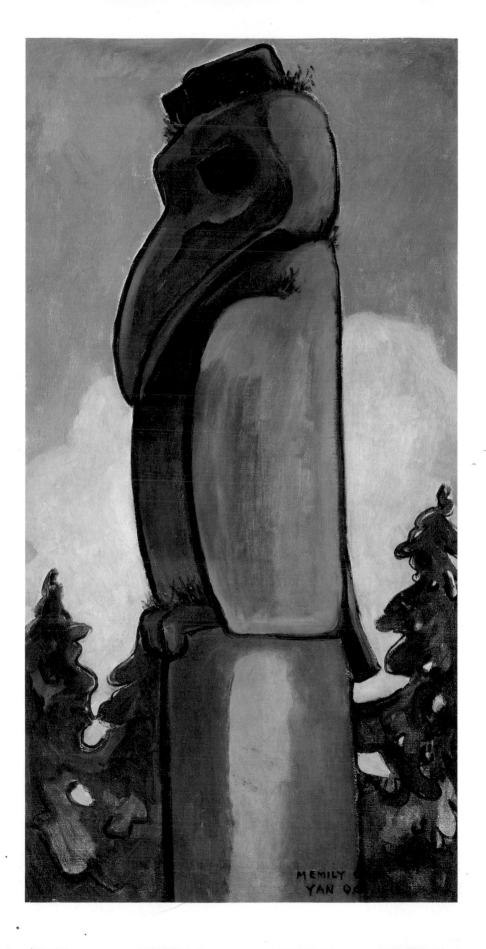

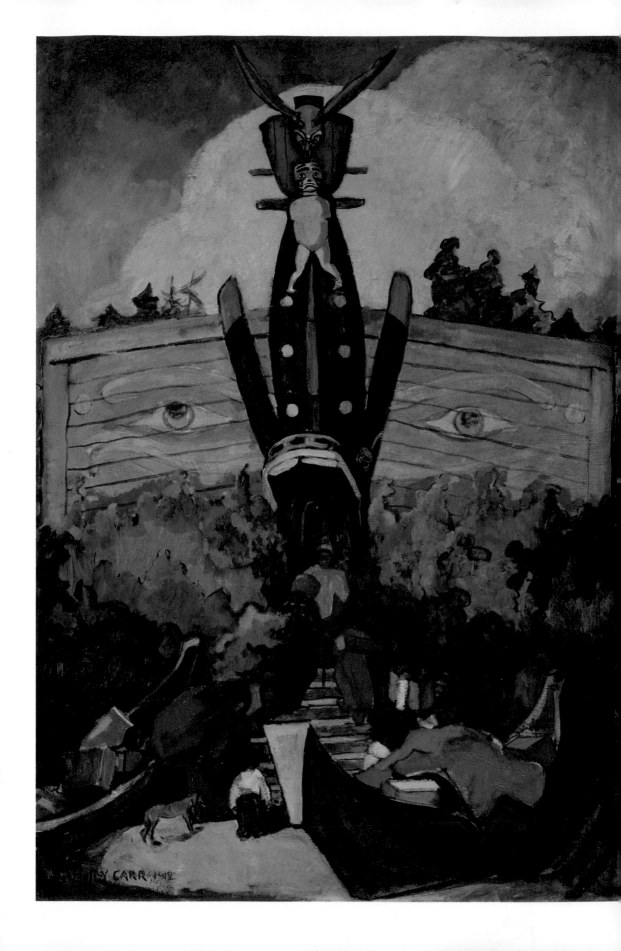

Indian Art broadened my seeing, loosened the formal tightness I had learned in England's schools. Its bigness and stark reality baffled my white man's understanding . . . I had been schooled to see outsides only, not struggle to pierce.

—Emily Carr, GROWING PAINS (THE EMILY CARR OMNIBUS, p. 427)

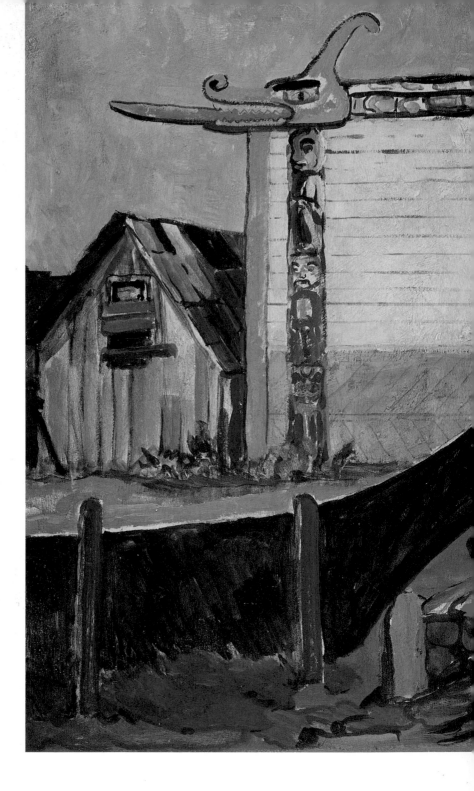

KWAKIUTL HOUSE
1912
oil on board
59.4 × 90.7 cm
Vancouver Art Gallery,
Emily Carr Trust,
42.3.33

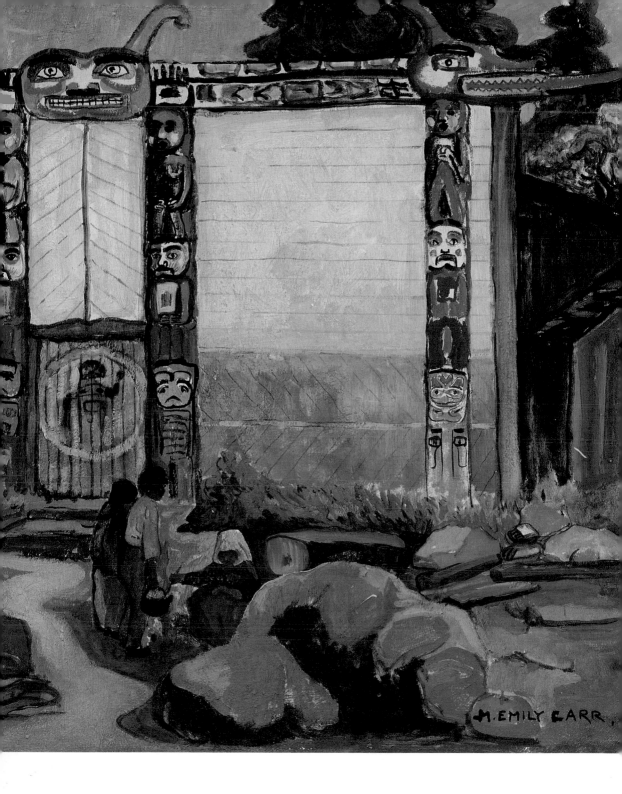

Went with Miss Buell and Mrs. Housser to tea at Mr. A. Y. Jackson's Studio
Building. I loved his things, particularly some snow things of Quebec and three
canvases up Skeena River. I felt a little as if beaten at my own game. His Indian
pictures have something mine lack—rhythm, poetry. Mine are so downright.
But perhaps his haven't quite the love in them of the people and the country that
mine have. How could they? He is not a Westerner and I took no liberties.
I worked for history and cold fact. Next time I paint Indians I'm going off on
a tangent tear. There is something bigger than fact: the underlying spirit, all it
stands for, the mood, the vastness, the wildness.

—Emily Carr, HUNDREDS AND THOUSANDS (THE EMILY CARR OMNIBUS, p. 656)

THREE TOTEMS
c. 1928-29
oil on canvas
109.0 × 69.4 cm
Vancouver Art Gallery,
Emily Carr Trust,
42.3.26

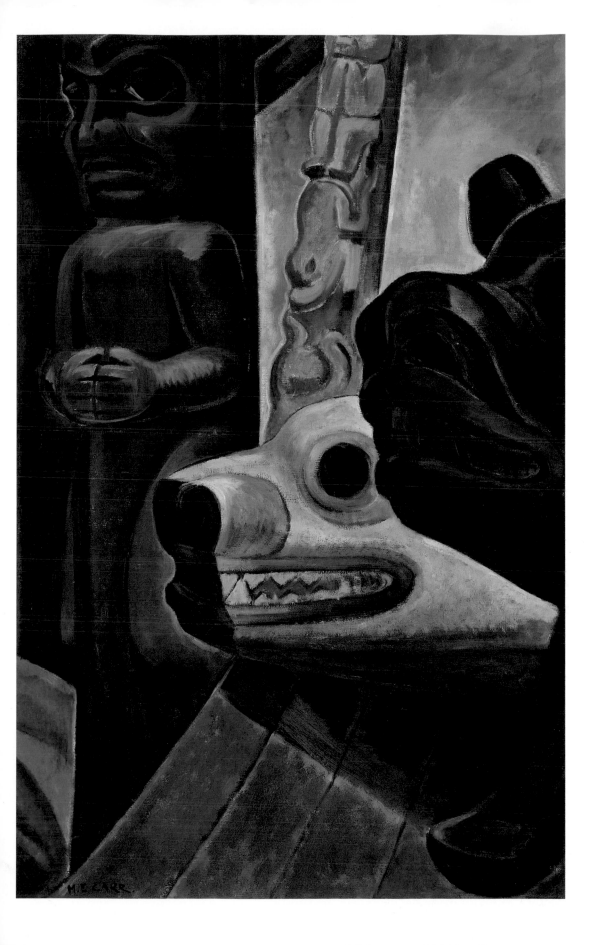

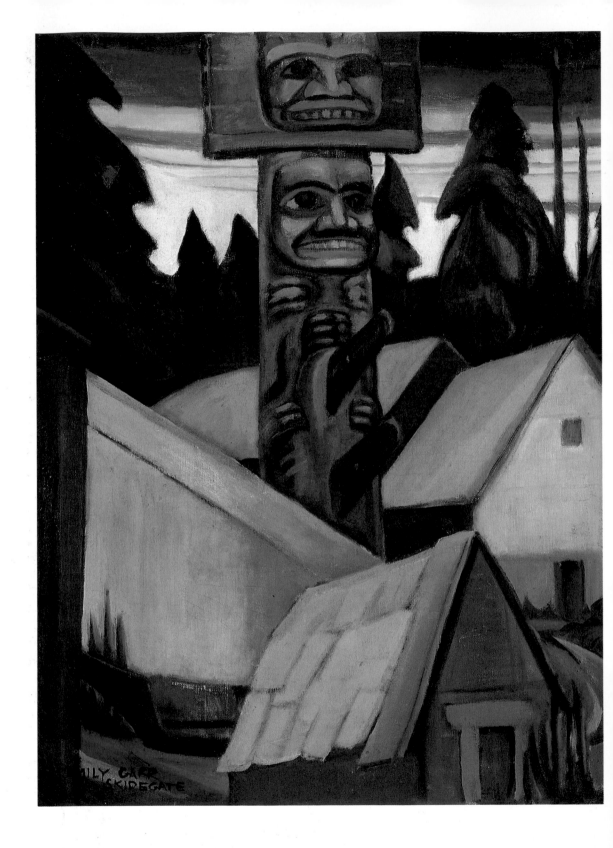

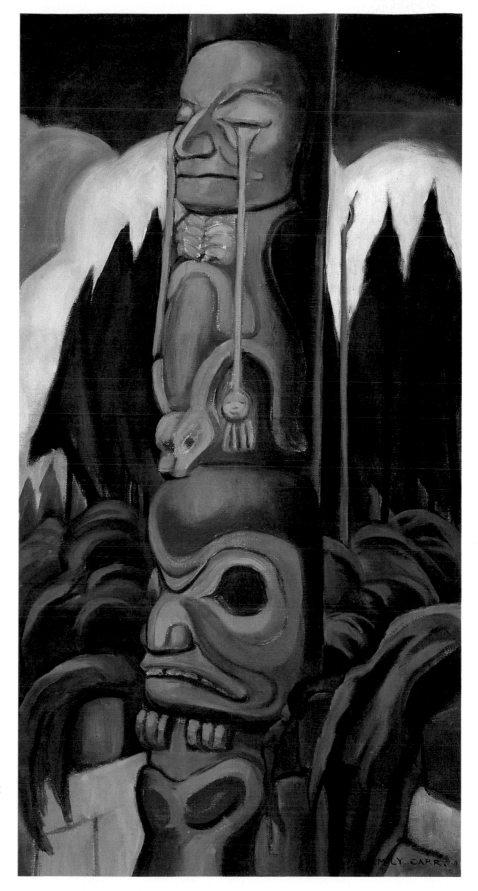

facing page:
SKIDEGATE 1928
oil on canvas
61.5 × 46.4 cm
Vancouver Art Gallery,
Emily Carr Trust,
42.3.48

this page:
THE CRYING TOTEM
1928
oil on canvas
75.3 × 38.8 cm
Vancouver Art Gallery,
Emily Carr Trust,
42.3.53

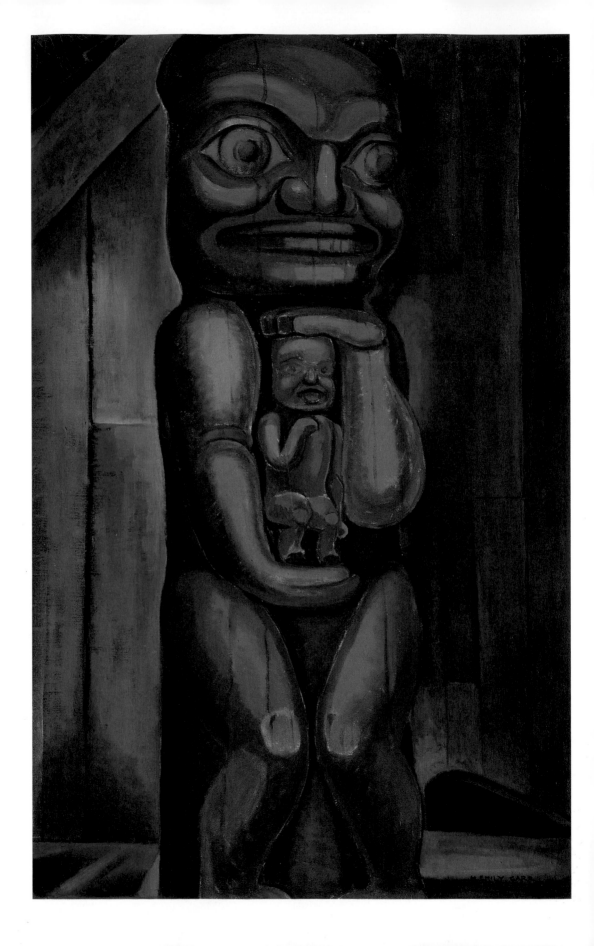

The sun enriched the old poles grandly. They were carved elaborately and with great sincerity. Several times the figure of a woman that held a child was represented The babies had faces like wise little old men. The mothers expressed all womanhood—the big wooden hands holding the child were so full of tenderness they had to be distorted enormously in order to contain it all. Womanhood was strong in Kitwancool.

—Emily Carr, KLEE WYCK (THE EMILY CARR OMNIBUS, p. 80)
* See Notes

TOTEM MOTHER,
KITWANCOOL 1928
oil on canvas
109.7 × 69.7 cm
Vancouver Art Gallery,
Emily Carr Trust,
42.3.20

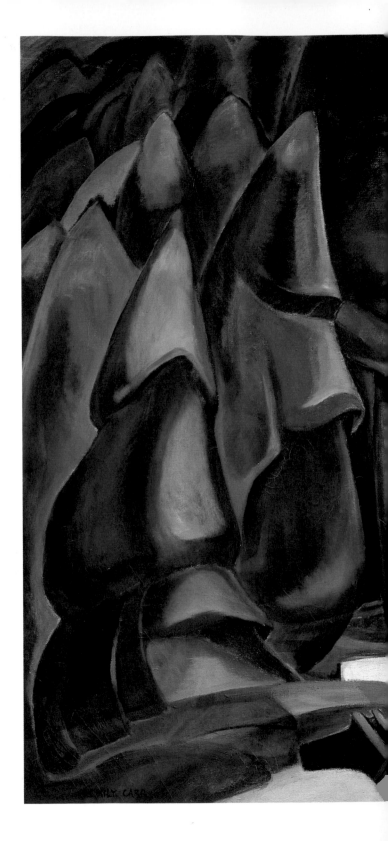

OLD TIME COAST
VILLAGE 1929-30
oil on canvas
91.3 × 128.7 cm
Vancouver Art Gallery,
Emily Carr Trust,
42.3.4

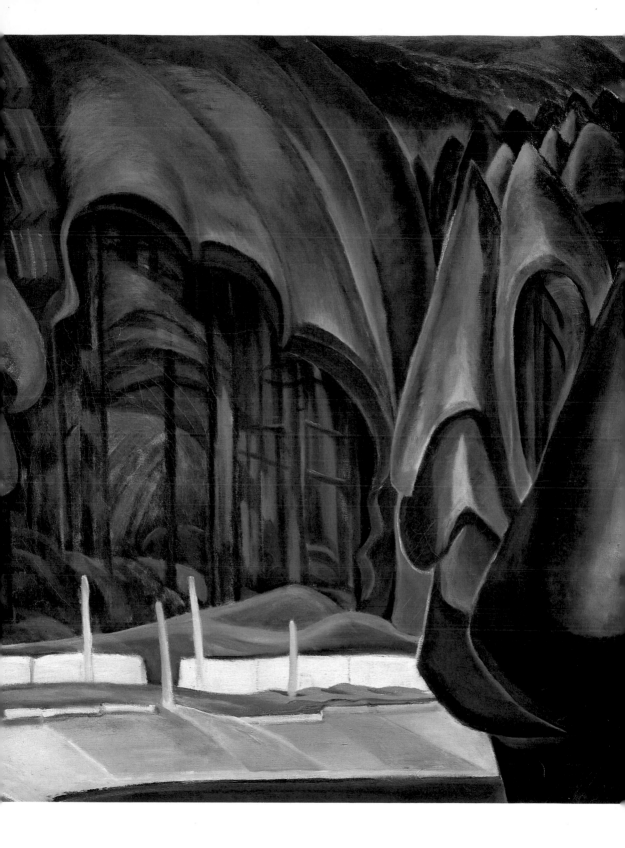

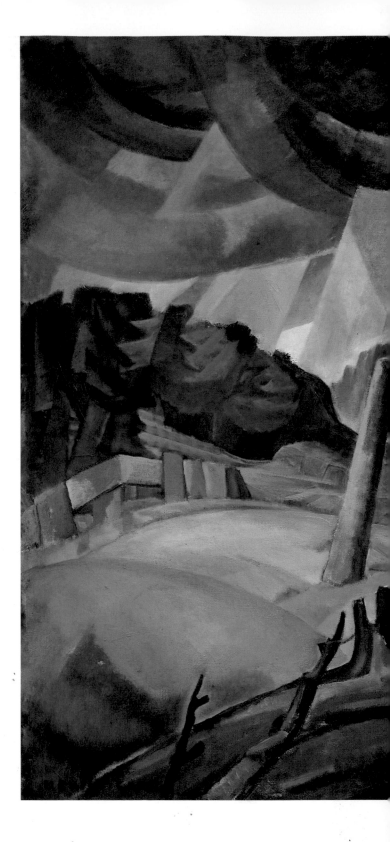

VANQUISHED 1930
oil on canvas
92.0 × 129.0 cm
Vancouver Art Gallery,
Emily Carr Trust,
42.3.6

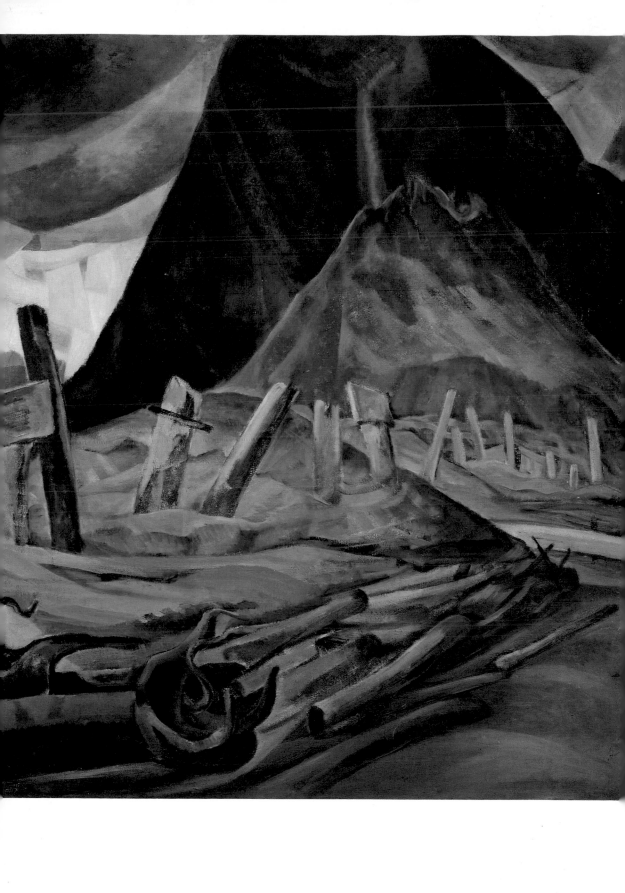

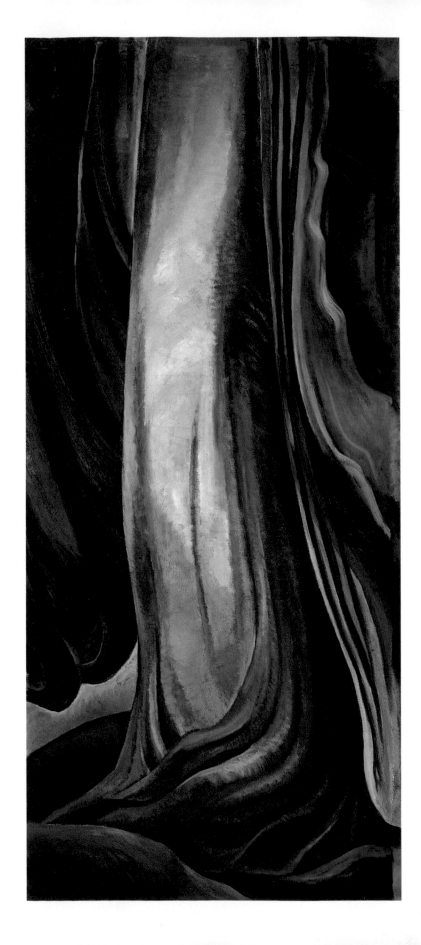

I went no more then to the far villages, but to the deep, quiet woods near home where I sat staring, staring, staring—half lost, learning a new language or rather the same language in a different dialect. So still were the big woods where I sat, sound might not yet have been born.

—Emily Carr, GROWING PAINS (THE EMILY CARR OMNIBUS, p. 444)

TREE TRUNK 1929-30
oil on canvas
129.1 × 56.3 cm
Vancouver Art Gallery,
Emily Carr Trust,
42.3.2

Not far from the house sat a great wooden raven mounted on a rather low pole; his wings were flattened to his sides. A few feet from him stuck up an empty pole. His mate had sat there but she had rotted away long ago, leaving him moss-grown, dilapidated and alone to watch dead Indian bones, for these two great birds had been set, one on either side of the doorway of a big house that had been full of dead Indians who had died during a smallpox epidemic.

Bursting growth had hidden house and bones long ago. Rain turned their dust into mud; these strong young trees were richer perhaps for that Indian dust. They grew up round the dilapidated old raven, sheltering him from the tearing winds now that he was old and rotting . . . The Cumshewa totem poles were dark and colourless, the wood toneless from pouring rain . . .

The memory of Cumshewa is of a great lonesomeness smothered in a blur of rain.

—Emily Carr, KLEE WYCK (THE EMILY CARR OMNIBUS, p. 33)

BIG RAVEN 1931
oil on canvas
87.3 × 114.4 cm
Vancouver Art Gallery,
Emily Carr Trust,
42.3.11

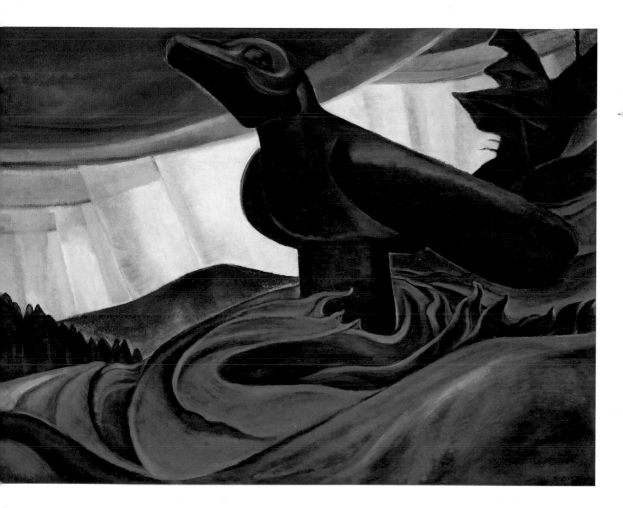

Like the D'Sonoqua of the other villages she was carved into the bole of a red cedar tree. Sun and storm had bleached the wood, moss here and there softened the crudeness of the modelling; sincerity underlay every stroke.

She appeared to be neither wooden nor stationary, but a singing spirit, young and fresh, passing through the jungle. No violence coarsened her; no power domineered to wither her. She was graciously feminine. Across her forehead her creator had fashioned the Sistheutl, or mythical two-headed sea-serpent. One of its heads fell to either shoulder, hiding the stuck-out ears, and framing her face from a central parting on her forehead which seemed to increase its womanliness.

She caught your breath, this D'Sonoqua, alive in the dead bole of the cedar. She summed up the depth and charm of the whole forest, driving away its menace.

I sat down to sketch. What was the noise of purring and rubbing going on about my feet? Cats. I rubbed my eyes to make sure I was seeing right, and counted a dozen of them. They jumped into my lap and sprang to my shoulders. They were real—and very feminine.

There we were—D'Sonoqua, the cats and I—the woman who only a few moments ago had forced herself to come behind the houses in trembling fear of the 'wild woman of the woods'—wild in the sense that forest-creatures are wild—shy, untouchable.

—Emily Carr, KLEE WYCK (THE EMILY CARR OMNIBUS, p. 44)
* See Notes

ZUNOQUA OF THE
CAT VILLAGE 1931
oil on canvas
112.5 × 70.5 cm
Vancouver Art Gallery,
Emily Carr Trust,
42.3.21

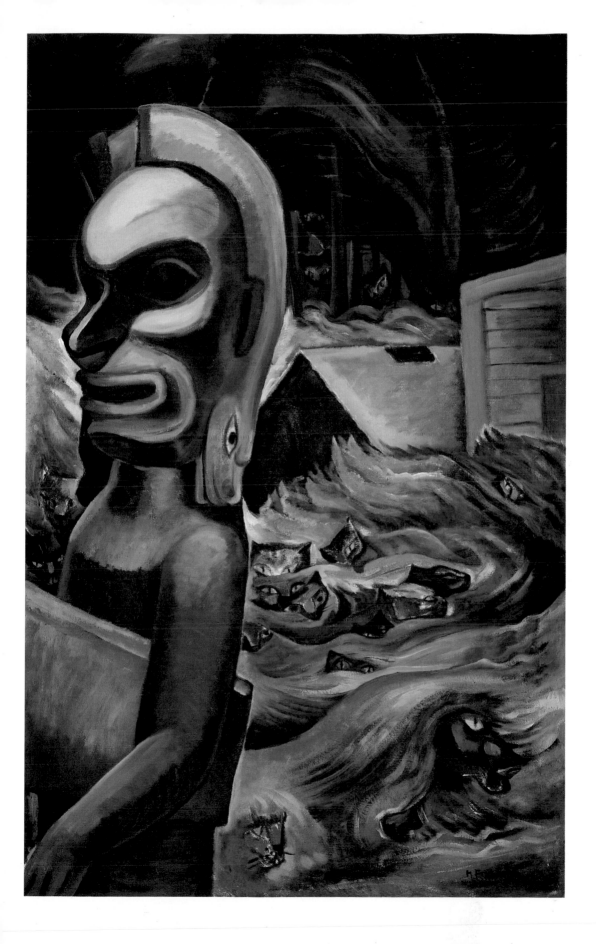

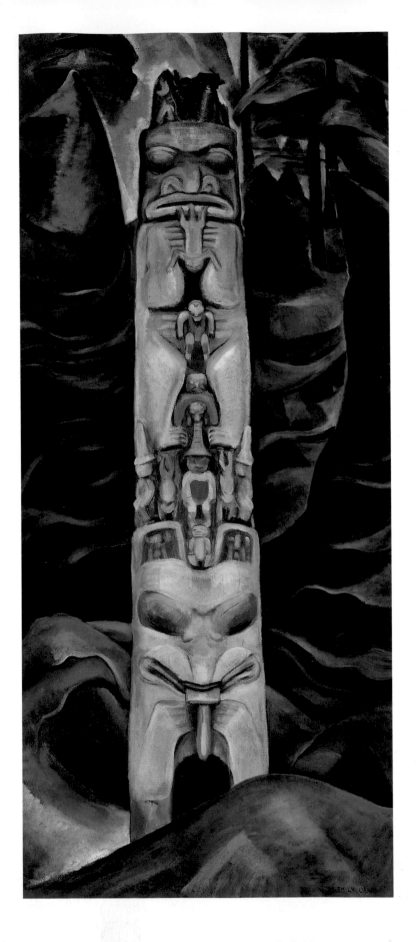

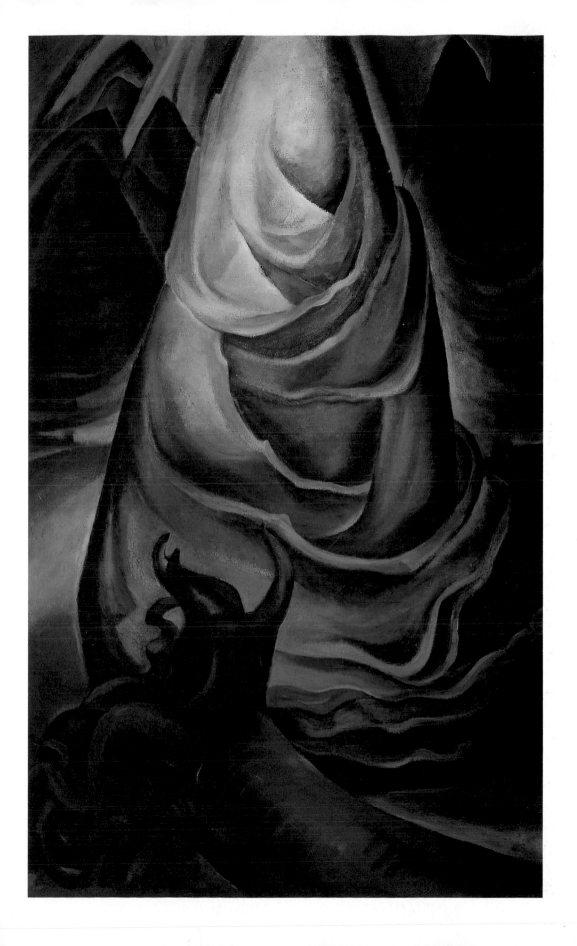

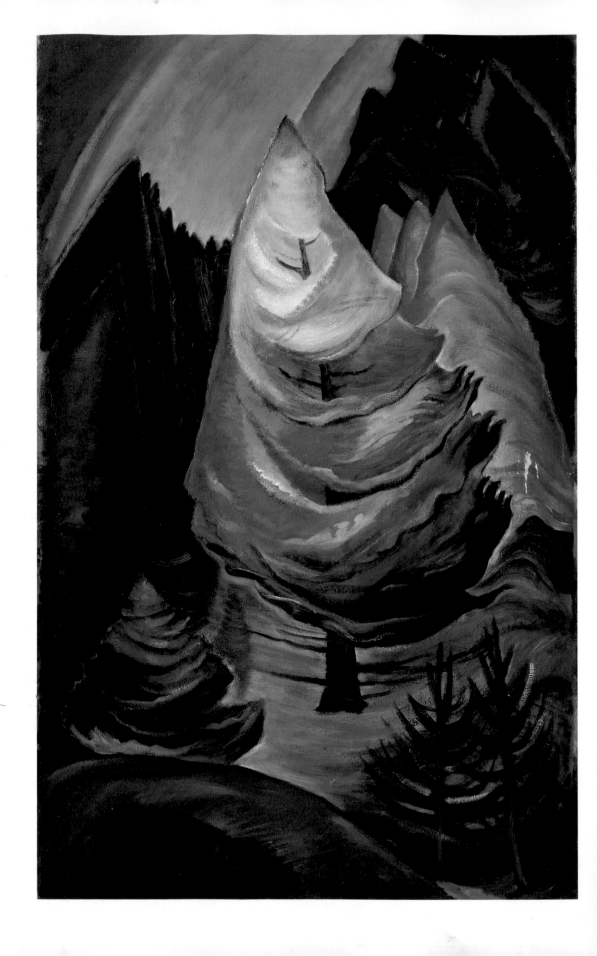

I have done a charcoal sketch today of young pines at the foot of a forest. I may take a canvas out of it. It should lead from joy back to mystery—young pines full of light and joyousness against a background of moving, mysterious forest. Last night I dreamed that I came face to face with a picture I had done and forgotten, a forest done in simple movement, just forms of trees moving in space. That is the third time I have seen pictures in my dreams, a glint of what I am striving to attain. Perhaps some day I shall get things clearer. Every day I long for the woods more, to get away and commune with things. Oh, Spring! I want to go out and feel you and get inspiration. My old things seem dead. I want fresh contacts, more vital searching.

—Emily Carr, HUNDREDS AND THOUSANDS (THE EMILY CARR OMNIBUS, p. 671)

THE LITTLE PINE
1931
oil on canvas
112.0 × 68.8 cm
Vancouver Art Gallery,
Emily Carr Trust,
42.3.14

This perhaps is the way to find that thing I long for: go into the woods alone and look at the earth crowded with growth, new and old bursting from their strong roots hidden in the silent, live ground, each seed according to its own kind expanding, bursting, pushing its way upward towards the light and air, each one knowing what to do, each one demanding its own rights on the earth. Feel this growth, the surging upward, this expansion, the pulsing life, all working with the same idea, the same urge to express the God in themselves . . . So, artist, you too from the deeps of your soul, down among dark and silence, let your roots creep forth, gaining strength. Draw deeply from the good nourishment of the earth but rise into the glory of the light and air and sunshine.

—Emily Carr, HUNDREDS AND THOUSANDS (THE EMILY CARR OMNIBUS, p. 676)

SEA DRIFT AT
THE EDGE OF THE
FOREST c. 1931
oil on canvas
68.9 × 117.8 cm
Vancouver Art Gallery,
Emily Carr Trust,
42.3.25

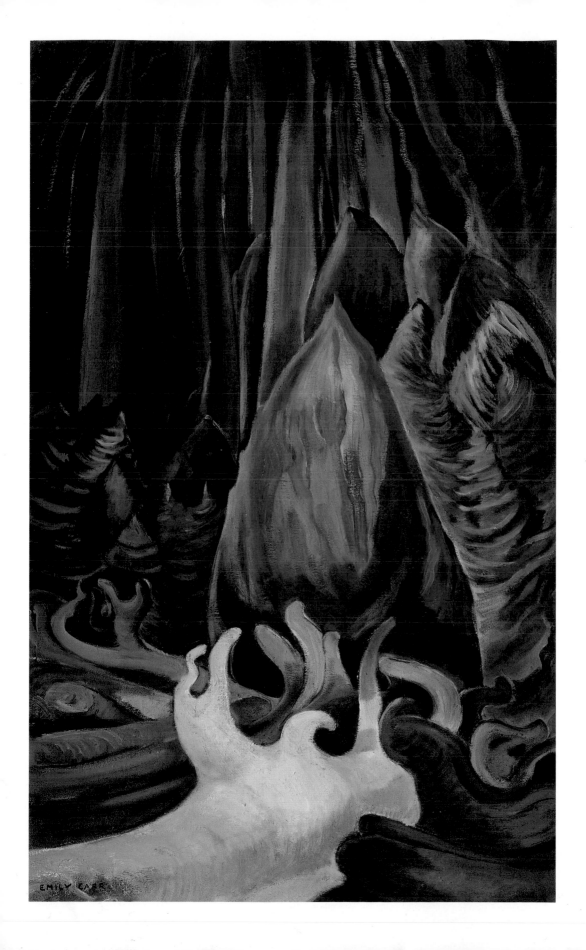

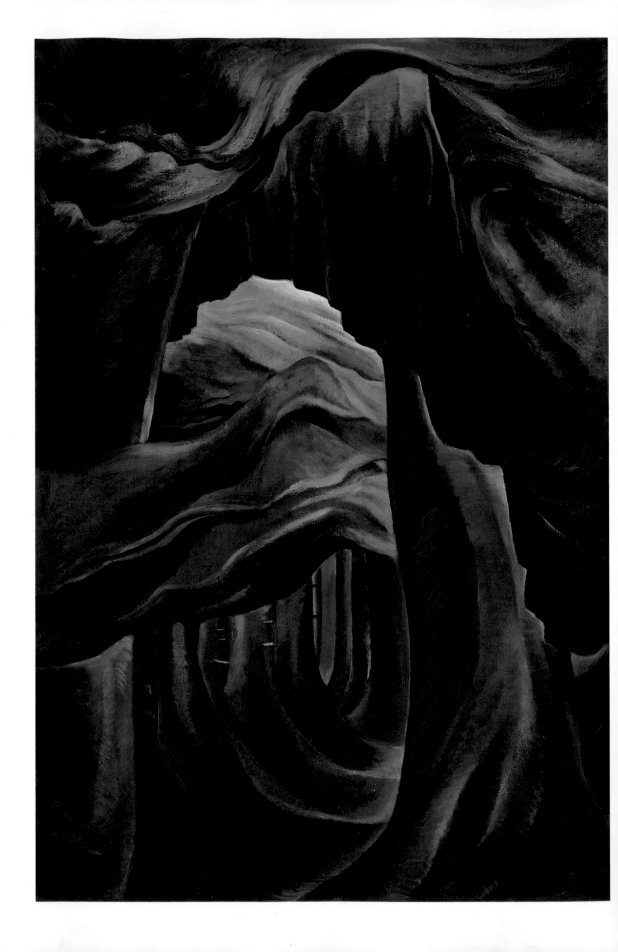

Go out there into the glory of the woods. See God in every particle of them expressing glory and strength and power, tenderness and protection. Know that they are God expressing God made manifest. Feel their protecting spread, their uplifting rise, their solid immovable strength. Regard the warm red earth beneath them nurtured by their myriads of fallen needles, softly fallen, slowly disintegrating through long processes, always living, changing, expanding round and round. It is a continuous process of life, eternally changing yet eternally the same. See God in it all, enter into the life of the trees. Know your relationship and understand their language, unspoken, unwritten talk. Answer back to them with their own dumb magnificence, soul words, earth words, the God in you responding to the God in them.

—Emily Carr, HUNDREDS AND THOUSANDS (THE EMILY CARR OMNIBUS, p. 675)

FOREST, BRITISH
COLUMBIA 1931-32
oil on canvas
130.0 × 86.8 cm
Vancouver Art Gallery,
Emily Carr Trust,
42.3.9

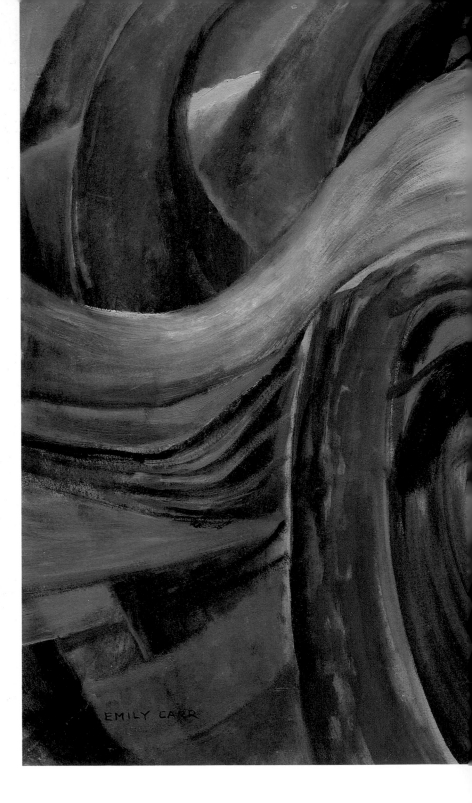

ABSTRACT TREE
FORMS 1931-32
oil on paper
60.0 × 90.0 cm
Vancouver Art Gallery,
Emily Carr Trust,
42.3.54

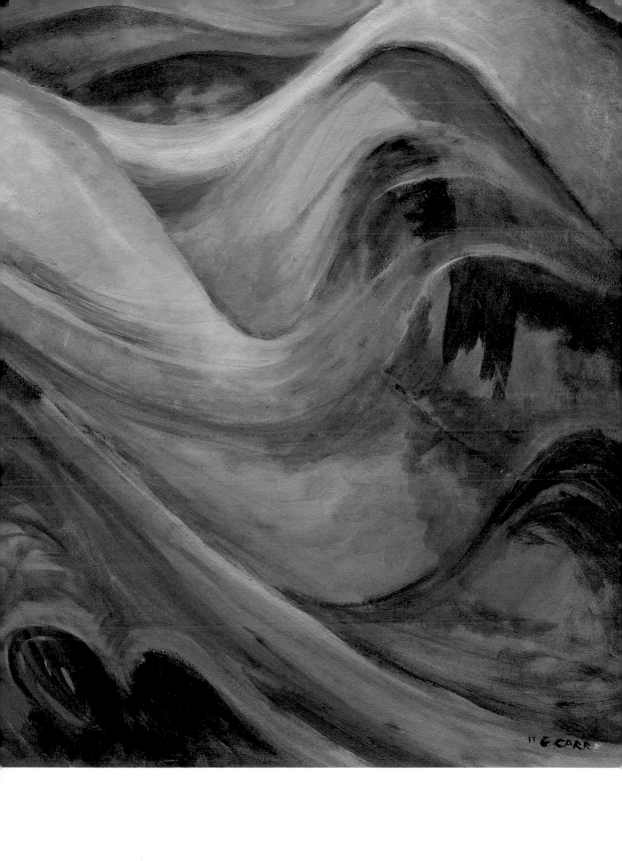

I was not ready for abstraction. I clung to earth and her dear shapes, her density, her herbage, her juice. I wanted her volume, and I wanted to hear her throb. I was tremendously interested in Lawren Harris's abstraction ideas, but I was not yet willing to accept them for myself.

—Emily Carr, GROWING PAINS (THE EMILY CARR OMNIBUS, p. 457)

UNTITLED c. 1931-32
oil on paper
45.6 × 30.0 cm
Vancouver Art Gallery,
Emily Carr Trust,
42.3.167

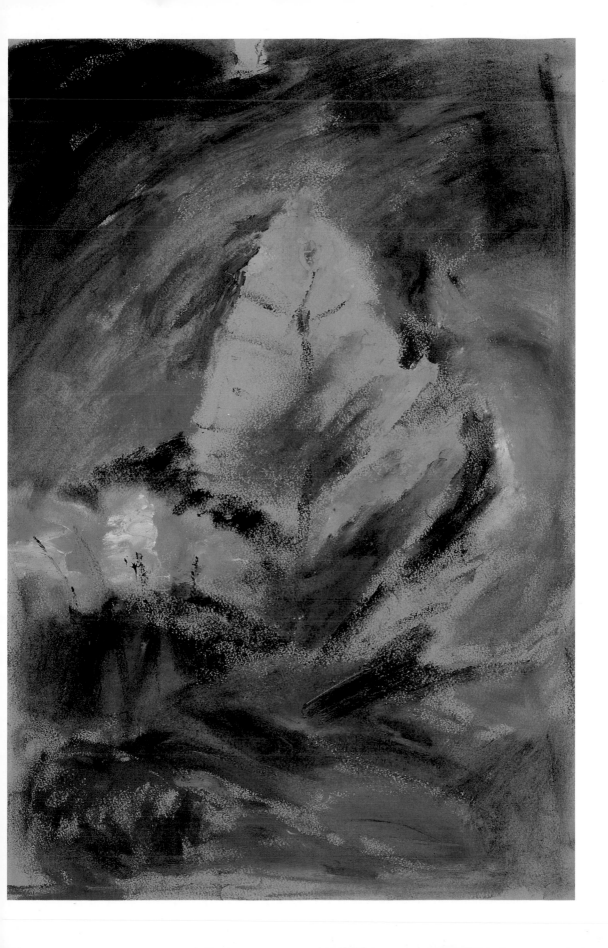

Woods you are very sly, picking those moments when you are quiet and off guard to reveal yourselves to us, folding us into your calm, accepting us to the sway, the rhythm of your spaces, space interwoven with the calm that rests forever in you.

For all that you stand so firmly rooted, so still, you quiver, there is movement in every leaf.

Woods you are not only a group of trees. Rather you are low space intertwined with growth.

Bless . . . the two painting masters who first pointed out to me (raw young pupil that I was) that there was coming and going among trees, that there was sunlight in shadows.

—Emily Carr, GROWING PAINS (THE EMILY CARR OMNIBUS, pp. 457-58)

FOREST 1931-33
oil on canvas
118.2 × 76.1 cm
Vancouver Art Gallery,
Emily Carr Trust,
42.3.13

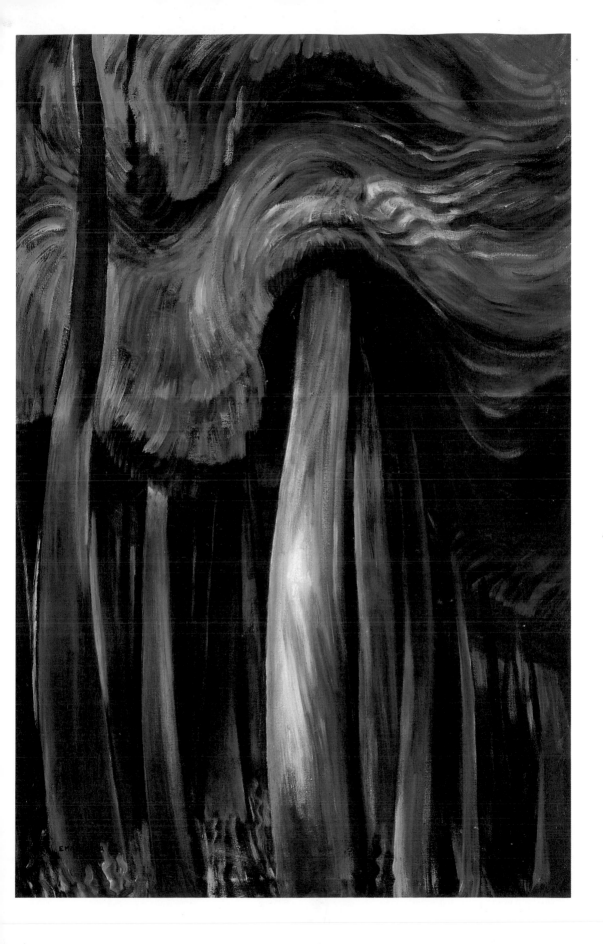

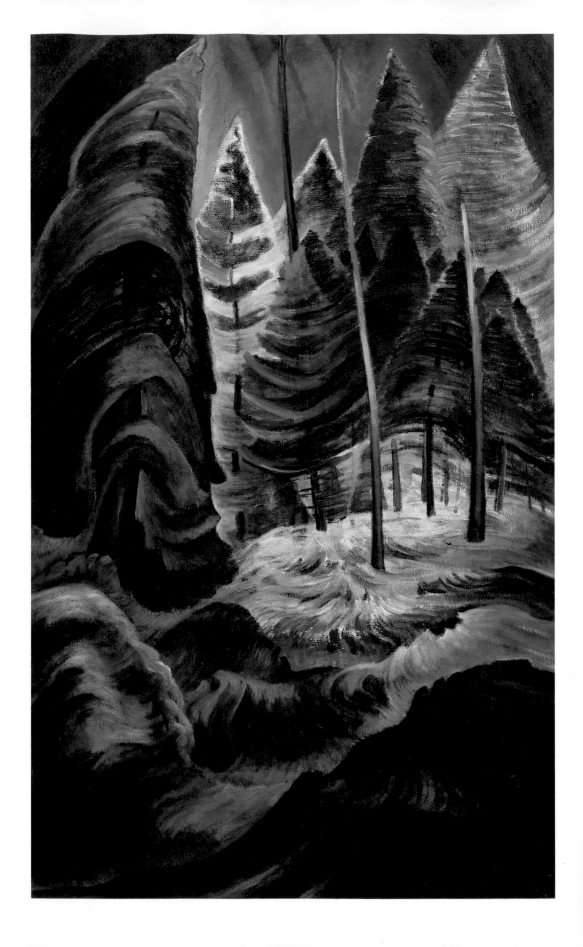

There is a sea of sallal and bracken, waving, surging, rolling towards you. Green jungle, thick yet loose-packed, solid, yet the very solidity full of air spaces. Perfectly ordered disorder designed with a helter-skelter magnificence. How can one express all this? To achieve it you must perch on a desperately uncomfortable log and dip among the roots for your material. Yet in spite of all the awkwardness there is a worthwhileness far exceeding a pretty sketch done at ease. There is a robust grandeur, loud-voiced, springing richly from earth untilled, unpampered, bursting forth rude, natural, without apology; an awful force greater in its stillness than the crashing, pounding sea, more akin to our own elements than water, defying man, offering to combat with him, pitting strength for strength, not racing like the sea to engulf, to drown you but inviting you to meet it, waiting for your advance, holding out gently swaying arms of invitation.

—Emily Carr, HUNDREDS AND THOUSANDS (THE EMILY CARR OMNIBUS, p. 798)

A RUSHING SEA
OF UNDERGROWTH
1932-35
oil on canvas
112.8 × 69.0 cm
Vancouver Art Gallery,
Emily Carr Trust,
42.3.17

There are no words, no paints to express all this, only a beautiful dumbness in the soul, life speaking to life. Down under the top greenery there is a mysterious space. From the eye-level of a camp stool you can peep in under. Once I went to some very beautiful children's exercises in a great open space. There was no grandstand. The ground was level and it was most difficult to see. I took a camp stool and when my feet gave out I sat down. It was very quiet down among the legs of the dense crowd . . . a forest of legs with no tops . . . Well, that is the way it feels looking through bracken stalks and sallal bushes. Their tops have rushed up agog to see the sun and the patient roots only get what they can suck down through those tough stems. Seems as if there is something most wonderful of all about a forest, especially one with deep, lush undergrowth.

—Emily Carr, HUNDREDS AND THOUSANDS (THE EMILY CARR OMNIBUS, p. 799)

WOOD INTERIOR
1932-35
oil on canvas
130.0 × 86.3 cm
Vancouver Art Gallery,
Emily Carr Trust,
42.3.5

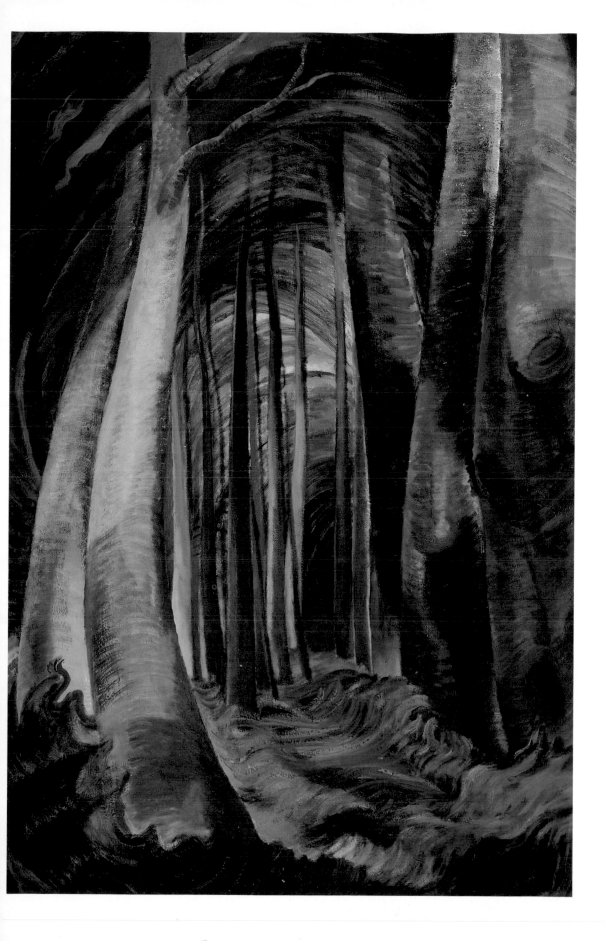

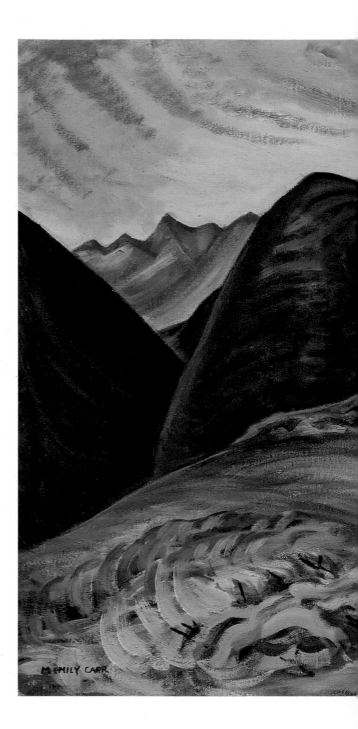

VILLAGE IN THE
HILLS 1933
oil on canvas
69.0 × 112.2 cm
Vancouver Art Gallery,
Emily Carr Trust,
42.3.22

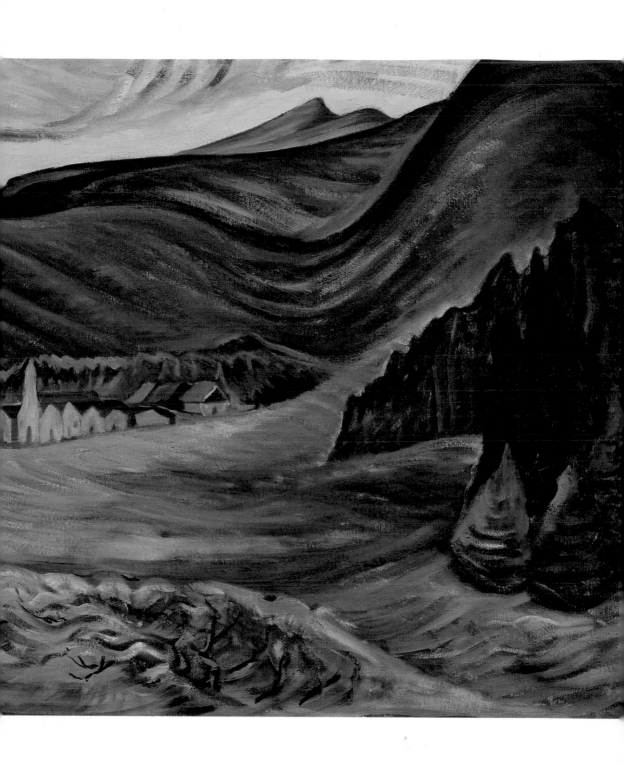

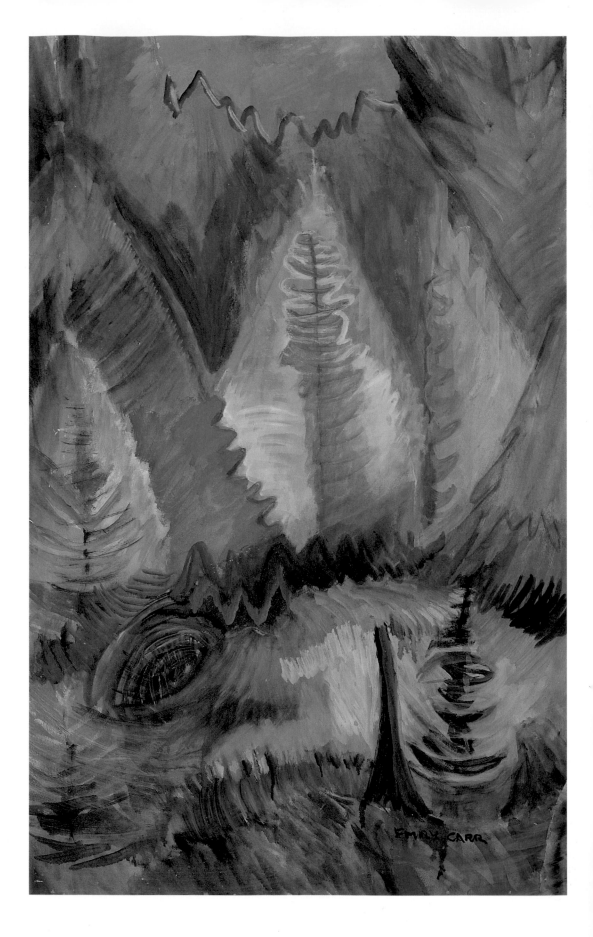

The sallal is tough and stubborn, rose and blackberry thorny. There are the fallen logs and mossy stumps, the thousand varieties of growth and shapes and obstacles, the dips and hollows, hillocks and mounds, riverbeds, forests of young pines and spruce piercing up through the tangle to get to the quiet light diluted through the overhanging branches of great overtopping trees. Should you sit down, the great, dry, green sea would sweep over and engulf you.

—Emily Carr, HUNDREDS AND THOUSANDS (THE EMILY CARR OMNIBUS, p. 804)

UNTITLED C. 1933-34
oil on paper
91.0 × 57.8 cm
Vancouver Art Gallery,
Emily Carr Trust,
42.3.79

My sketches have zip to them but they don't strike bottom yet. They move some but I want them to swell and roll back and forth into space, pausing here and there to fill out the song, catch the rhythm, to go down into the deep places and pause there and to rise up into the high ones, exulting. Let the movement be slow and savour of solidity at the base and rise quivering to the tree tops and to the sky, always rising to meet it joyously and tremulously. The objects before one are not enough, nor colour, nor form, nor design, nor composition. If spirit does not breathe through, it is lifeless, dead, voiceless. And the spirit must be felt so intensely that it has power to call others in passing, for it must pass, not stop in the pictures but be perpetually moving through, carrying on and inducing a thirst for more and a desire to rise.

—Emily Carr, HUNDREDS AND THOUSANDS (THE EMILY CARR OMNIBUS, p. 754)

FOREST EDGE AND SKY
c. 1934
oil on paper
91.2 × 61.4 cm
Vancouver Art Gallery,
Emily Carr Trust,
42.3.65

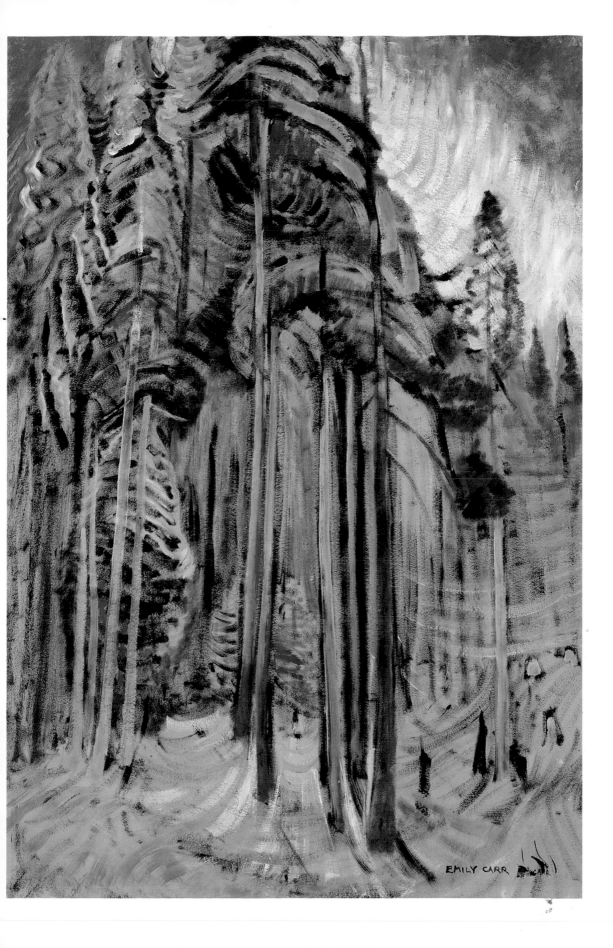

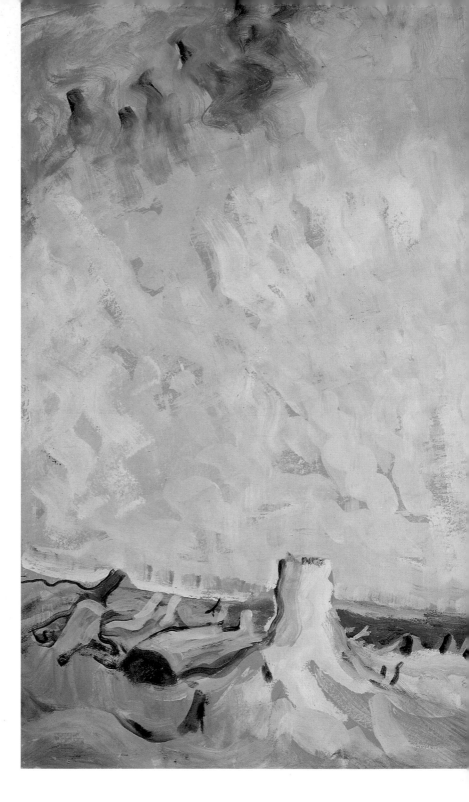

STUMPS AND SKY
c. 1934
oil on paper
59.5 × 90.0 cm
Vancouver Art Gallery,
Emily Carr Trust,
42.3.66

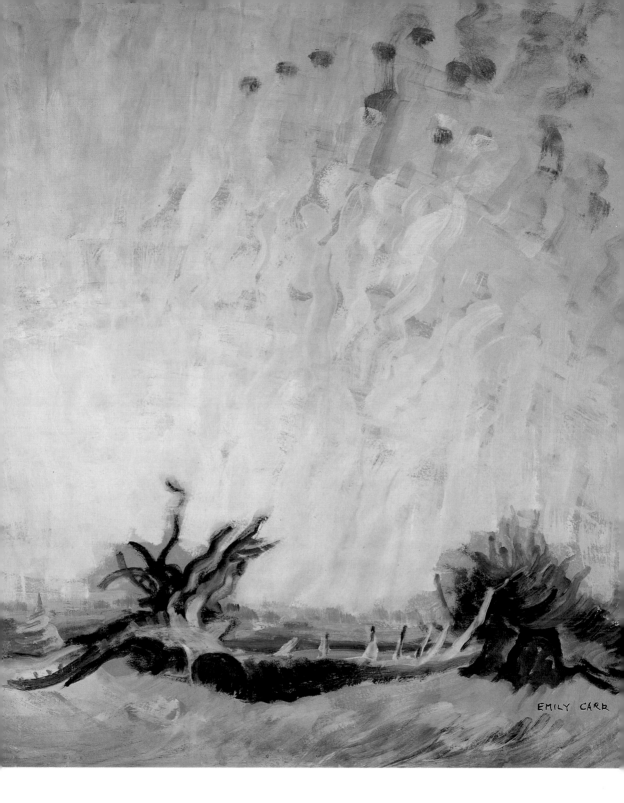

There's a row of pine trees that won't leave me alone. They are straight across the field from the van. Second growth, pointed, fluffy and thick ... They are very green, and sky, high and blue, is behind them. On days like today the relation-ship between the trees and the sky is very close. That, I think, is what makes a picture, a thought so expressed that the relationship of all the objects is shown to be in their right place. I used to paint a picture and stick in an interesting sky with clouds etc. that would decoratively balance my composition. It wasn't part of the conception of the whole. Now I know that the sky is just as important as the earth and the sea in working out the thought.

—Emily Carr, HUNDREDS AND THOUSANDS (THE EMILY CARR OMNIBUS, p. 789)

YOUNG PINES
AND SKY c. 1935
oil on paper
89.2 × 58.3 cm
Vancouver Art Gallery,
Emily Carr Trust,
42.3.80

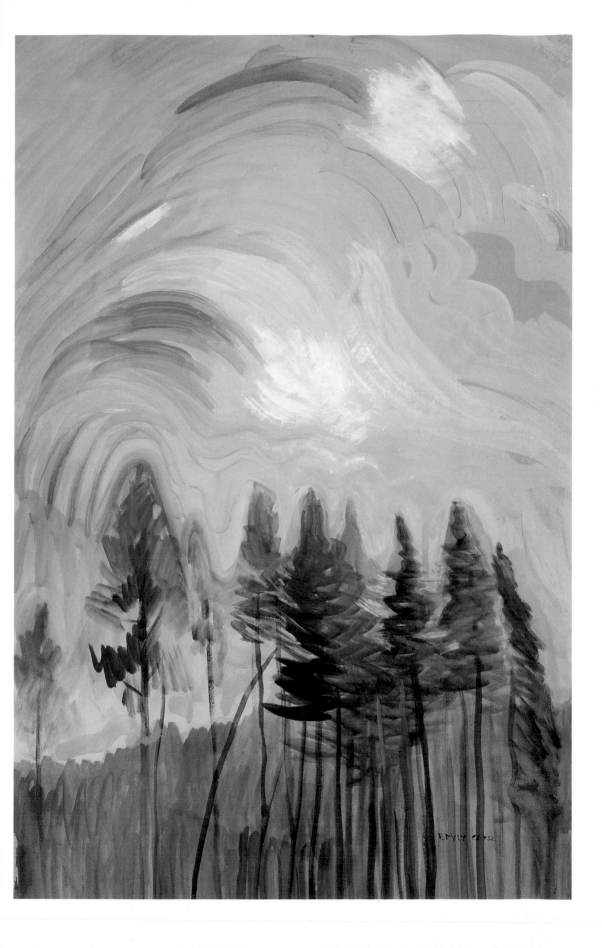

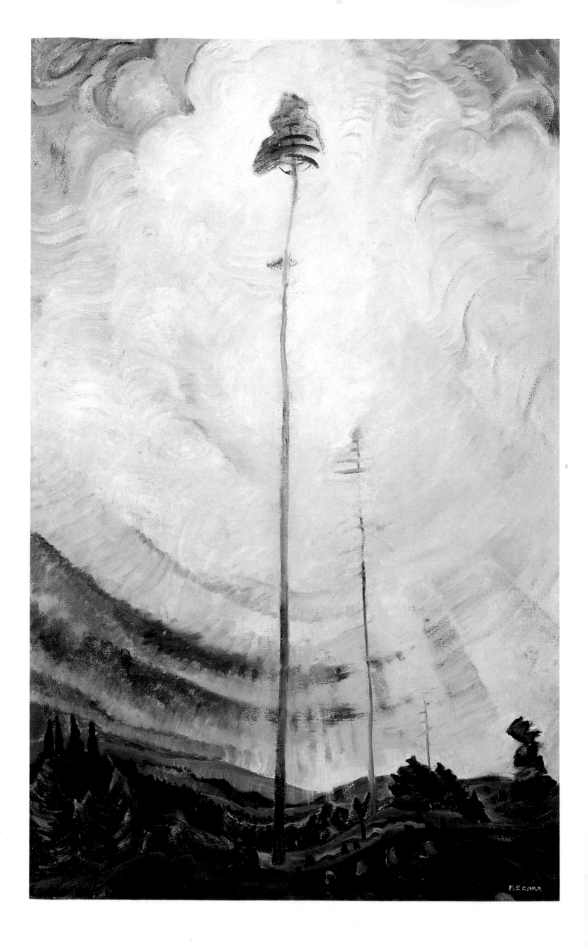

This is a place of high skies, blue and deep and seldom cloudless. I have been trying to express them and made a poor fist of it. Everything is eternally on the quiver with wind. It runs on the short dry grass and sluices it as if the earth were a jelly. The trees in shelter stand looking at the wobbly ones in the wind's path, like a strange pup watches two chum pups playing, a little enviously. I think trees love to toss and sway; they make such happy noises.

—Emily Carr, HUNDREDS AND THOUSANDS (THE EMILY CARR OMNIBUS, p. 789)

SCORNED AS
TIMBER, BELOVED
OF THE SKY 1935
oil on canvas
112.0 × 68.9 cm
Vancouver Art Gallery,
Emily Carr Trust,
42.3.15

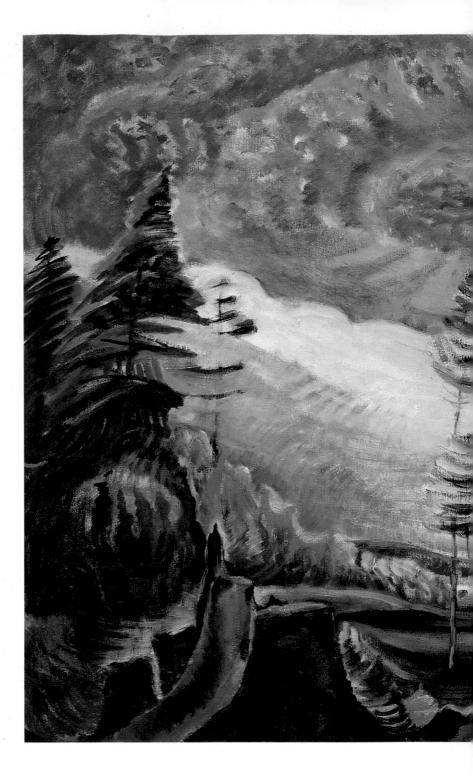

LOGGER'S CULLS 1935
oil on canvas
69.0 × 112.2 cm
Vancouver Art Gallery,
gift of Miss I. Parkyn,
39.1

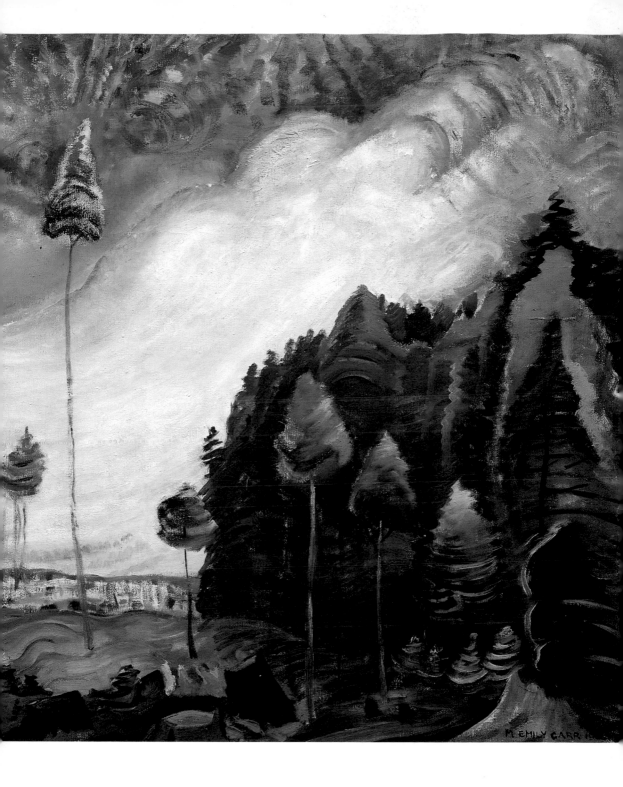

Life is sweeping through the spaces. Everything is alive. The air is alive. The silence is full of sound. The green is full of colour. Light and dark chase each other. Here is a picture, a complete thought, and there another and there . . .

There are themes everywhere, something sublime, something ridiculous, or joyous, or calm, or mysterious. Tender youthfulness laughing at gnarled oldness. Moss and ferns, and leaves and twigs, light and air, depth and colour chattering, dancing a mad joy-dance, but only apparently tied up in stillness and silence. You must be still in order to hear and see.

—Emily Carr, HUNDREDS AND THOUSANDS (THE EMILY CARR OMNIBUS, p. 794)

MOUNTAIN FOREST
1935-36
oil on canvas
112.0 × 67.0 cm
Vancouver Art Gallery,
Emily Carr Trust,
42.3.27

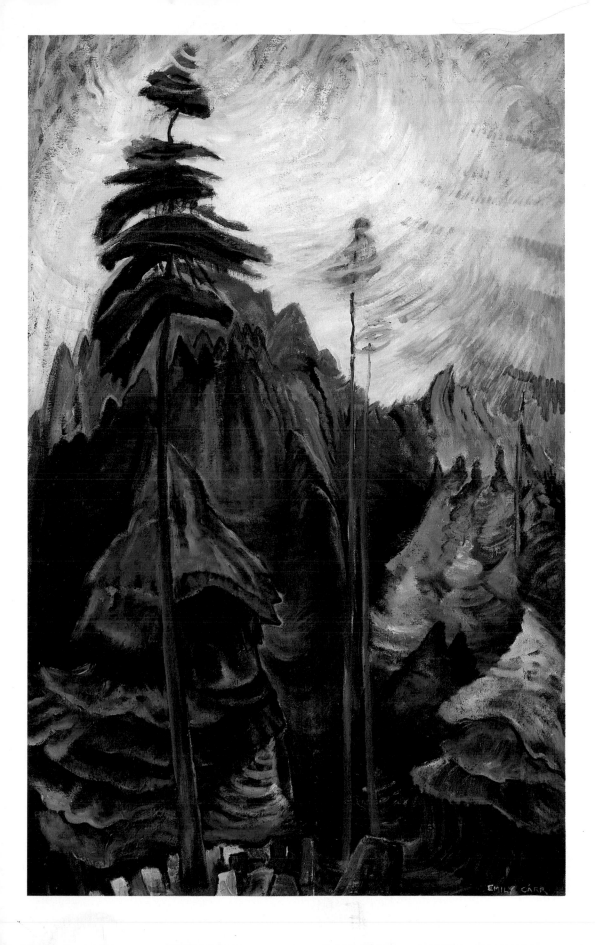

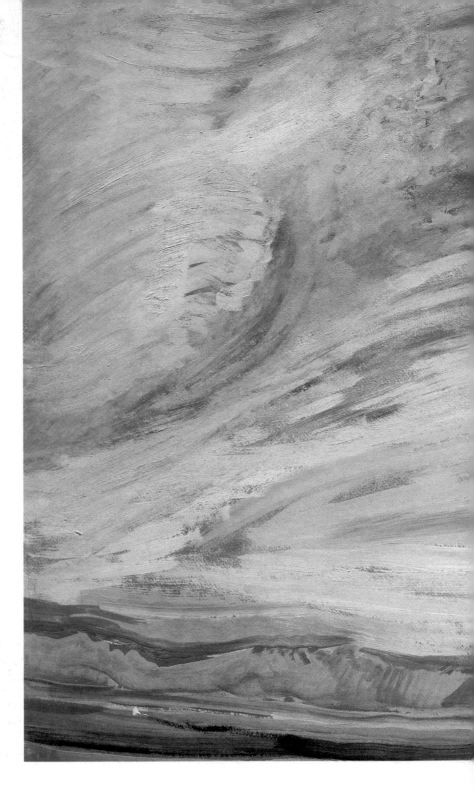

OVERHEAD 1935-36
oil on paper
61.0 × 91.0 cm
Vancouver Art Gallery,
Emily Carr Trust,
42.3.69

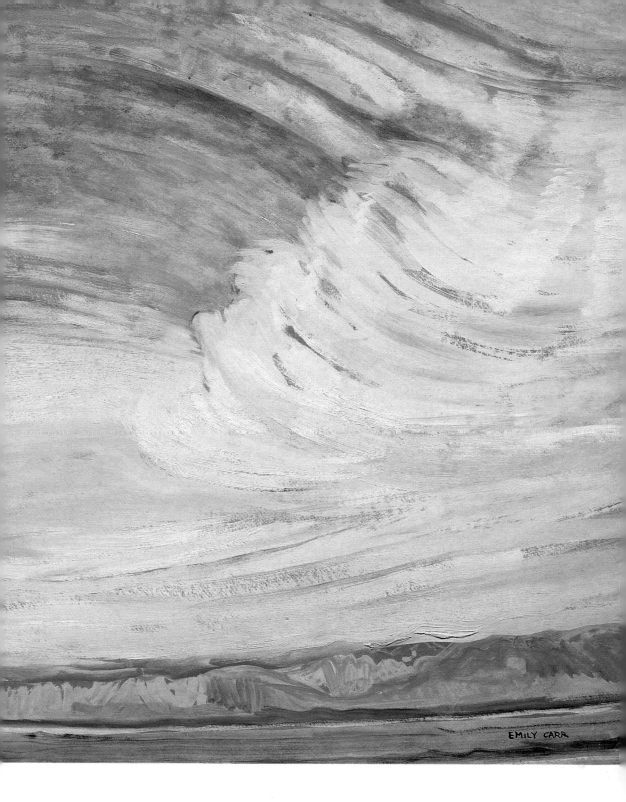
EMILY CARR

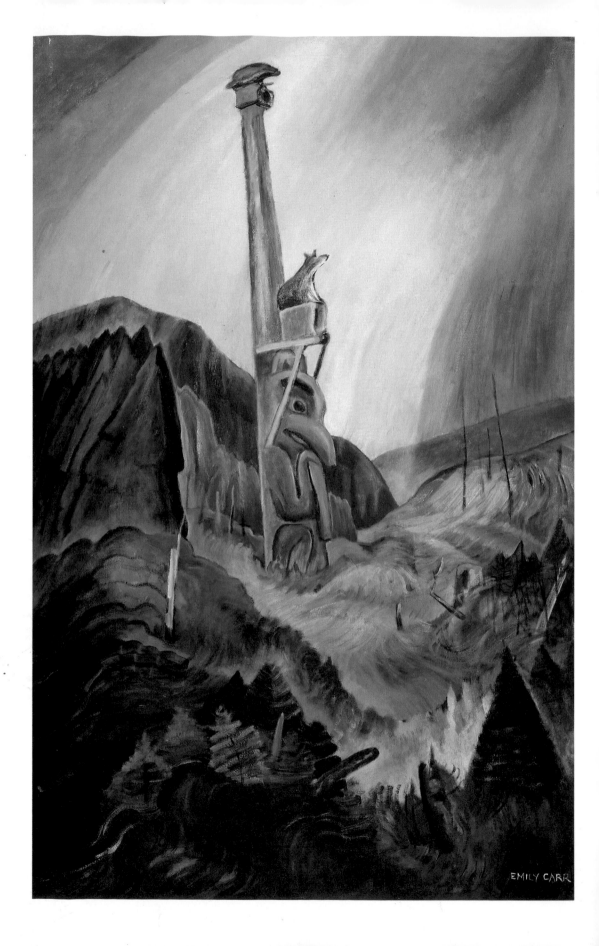

I have been painting all day, with four canvases on the go—Nass pole in undergrowth, Koskimo, Massett bear, and an exultant wood. My interest is keen and
the work of fair quality. I have been sent more ridiculous press notices. People are
frequently comparing my work with Van Gogh. Poor Van Gogh! . . . I do hope I
do not get bloated and self-satisfied. When proud feelings come I step up over
them to the realm of work, to the thing I want, the liveness of the thing itself.

—Emily Carr, HUNDREDS AND THOUSANDS (THE EMILY CARR OMNIBUS, pp. 861-62)

FORSAKEN c. 1932-37
oil on canvas
119.1 × 76.5 cm
Vancouver Art Gallery,
Emily Carr Trust,
42.3.12

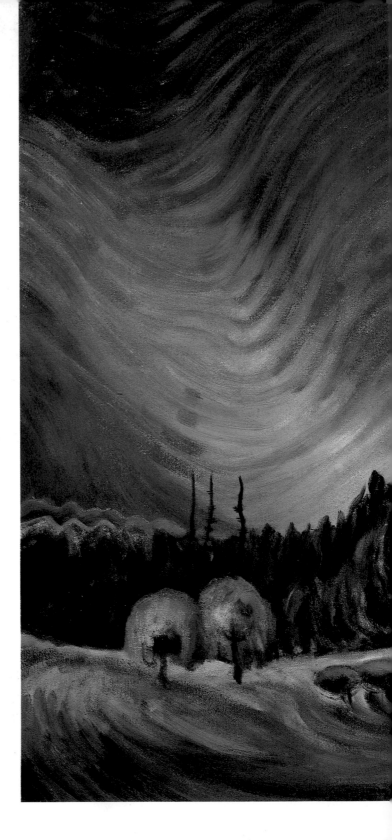

ABOVE THE
GRAVEL PIT 1936-37
oil on canvas
77.2 × 102.3 cm
Vancouver Art Gallery,
Emily Carr Trust,
42.3.30

98

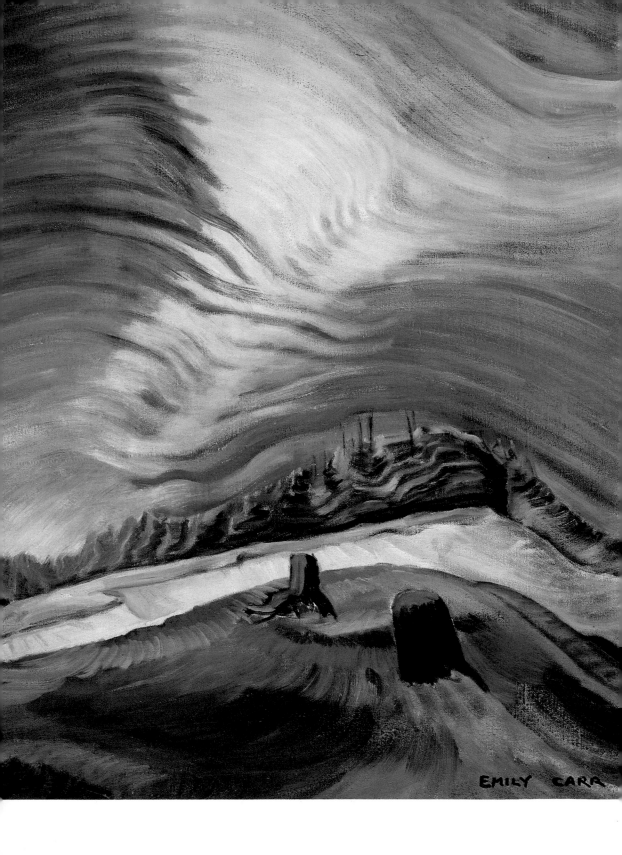

How badly I want that nameless thing! First there must be an idea, a feeling, or whatever you want to call it, the something that interested or inspired you sufficiently to make you desire to express it. Maybe it was an abstract idea that you've got to find a symbol for, or maybe it was a concrete form that you have to simplify or distort to meet your ends, but that starting point must pervade the whole. Then you must discover the pervading direction, the pervading rhythm, the dominant, recurring forms, the dominant colour, but always the thing must be top in your thoughts. Everything must lead up to it, clothe it, feed it, balance it, tenderly fold it, till it reveals itself in all the beauty of its idea.

—Emily Carr, HUNDREDS AND THOUSANDS (THE EMILY CARR OMNIBUS, pp. 671-72)

ABOVE THE TREES
1935- C. 1939
oil on paper
91.2 × 61.0 cm
Vancouver Art Gallery,
Emily Carr Trust,
42.3.83

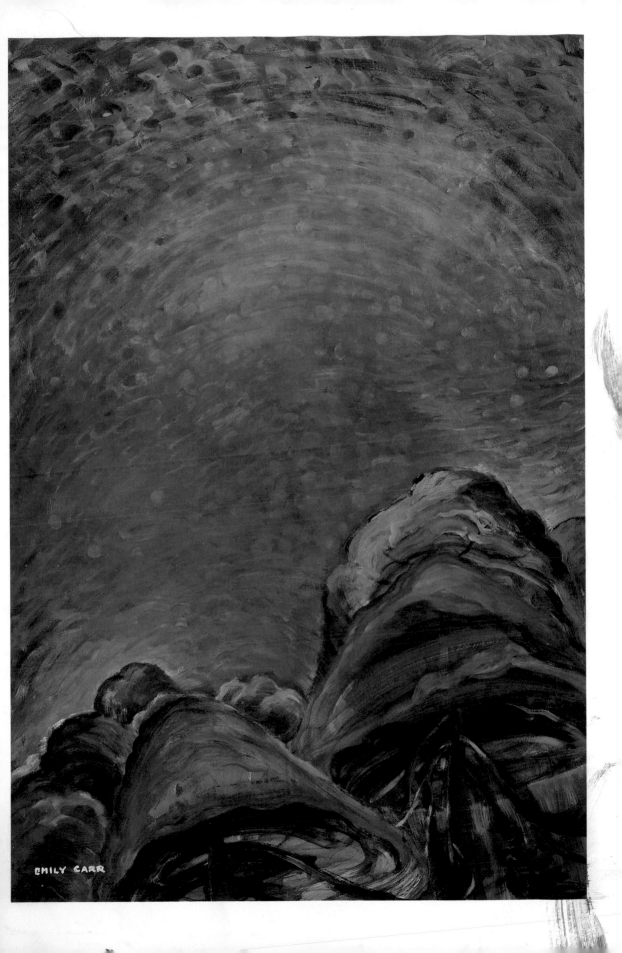

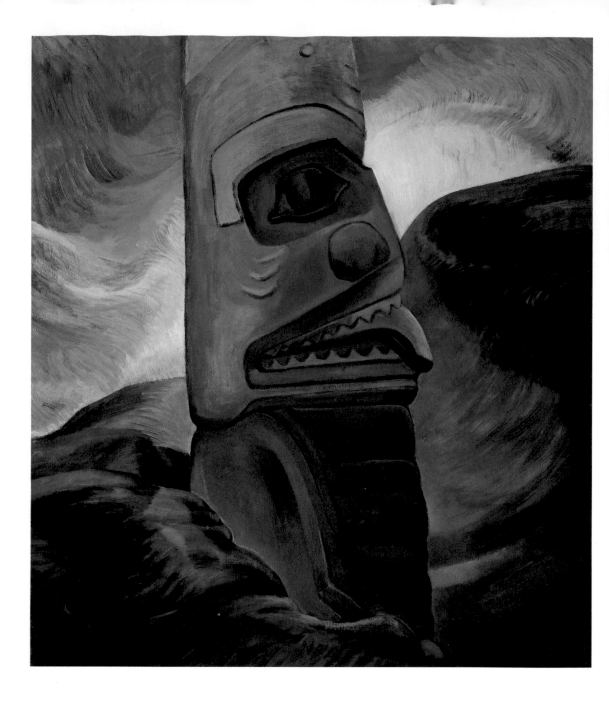

A SKIDEGATE POLE
1941-42
oil on canvas
87.0 × 76.5 cm
Vancouver Art Gallery,
Emily Carr Trust,
42.3.37

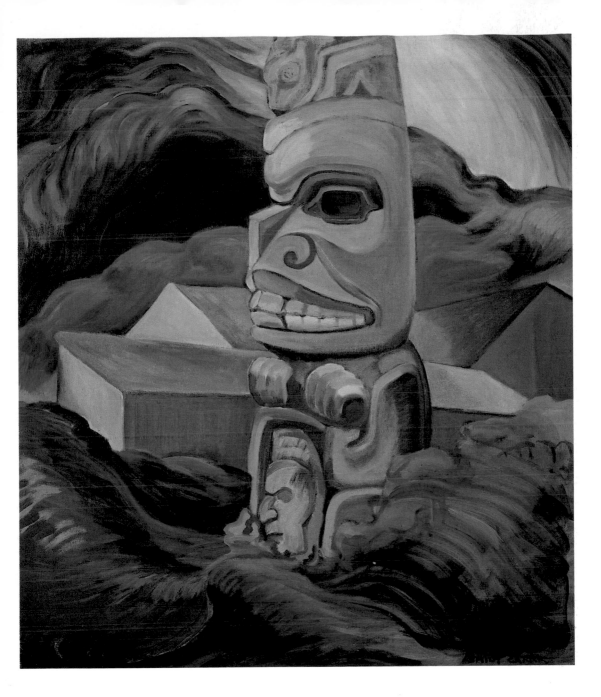

A SKIDEGATE
BEAVER POLE
1941-42
oil on canvas
86.0 × 76.3 cm
Vancouver Art Gallery,
Emily Carr Trust,
42.3.38

This place is full of cedars. Their colours are terribly sensitive to change of time and light—sometimes they are bluish cold green, then they turn yellow warm-green—sometimes their [boughs] flop heavy and sometimes float, then they are fairy as ferns and then they droop, heavy as heartaches.

—Emily Carr, 1942 letter to Ira Dilworth (quoted by Doris Shadbolt in
  THE ART OF EMILY CARR, p. 218)

CEDAR 1942
oil on canvas
112.0 × 69.0 cm
Vancouver Art Gallery,
Emily Carr Trust,
42.3.28

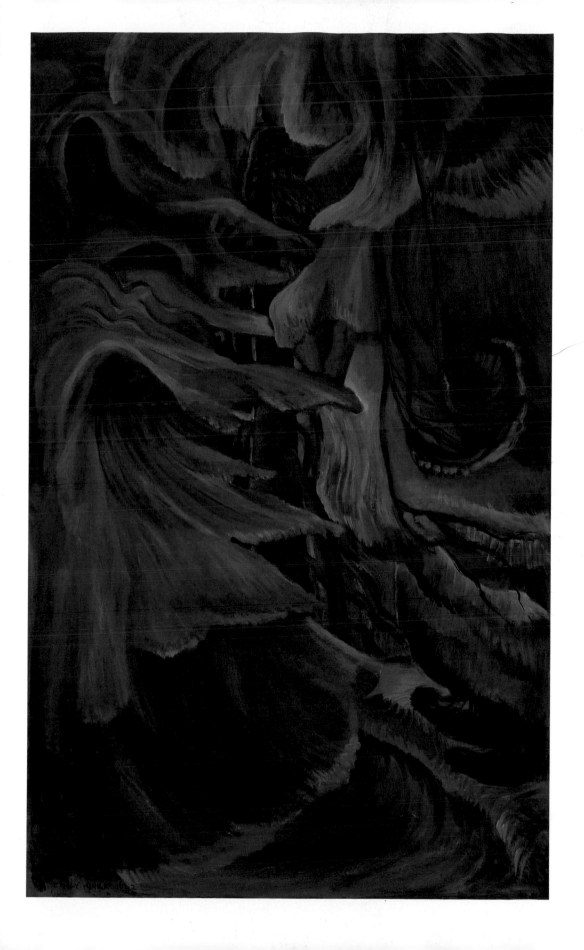

More than ever was I convinced that the old way of seeing was inadequate to express this big country of ours, her depth, her height, her unbounded wideness, silences too strong to be broken—nor could ten million cameras, through their mechanical boxes, ever show real Canada. It had to be sensed, passed through live minds, sensed and loved.

—Emily Carr, GROWING PAINS (THE EMILY CARR OMNIBUS, p. 437)

NOTES

Page 6 She expresses much of herself: Paula Blanchard, *The Life of Emily Carr* (Vancouver/Toronto: Douglas & McIntyre, 1987), 10; Doris Shadbolt, *Emily Carr* (Vancouver/Toronto: Douglas & McIntyre, 1990), 21.

6 Emily Carr altered the facts: Doris Shadbolt, *Emily Carr* (Vancouver/Toronto: Douglas & McIntyre, 1990), 21.

6 She found churches "stuffy": Emily Carr, *Hundreds and Thousands* in *The Emily Carr Omnibus*, ed. Doris Shadbolt (Vancouver/Toronto: Douglas & McIntyre, 1993), 891.

6 Although it caused her pain: Doris Shadbolt, *Emily Carr,* 24.

6 As Emily Carr told it: Emily Carr, *Growing Pains* in *The Emily Carr Omnibus*, ed. Doris Shadbolt (Vancouver/Toronto: Douglas & McIntyre, 1993), 301.

7 Richard Carr was: *Ibid.*

7 She professed to feel: Emily Carr, unpublished journals, quoted in Blanchard, *The Life of Emily Carr,* 58.

8 Looking back on her childhood: Emily Carr, *Growing Pains*, 307.

8 Significant during this expedition: Blanchard, *The Life of Emily Carr,* 291.

9 At the same time: Shadbolt, *Emily Carr*, 87.

9 He understood her aversion: Carr, *Growing Pains*, 402.

9 Although she was years away: Emily Carr, MS of *Growing Pains*, quoted in Blanchard, *The Life of Emily Carr,* 87.

10 Some believe that her symptoms: Maria Tippett, *Emily Carr: A Biography* (Toronto: Stoddart, 1994), 58.

10 Others suggest that: Blanchard, *The Life of Emily Carr,* 91.

11 Laboured and unlimber: *Ibid.,* 104.

11 The other important theme: Carr, *Growing Pains*, 425.

11 She sketched excitedly: Shadbolt, *Emily Carr*, 89.

11 Emily Carr resolved: Carr, *Growing Pains*, 427.

11 It was a bold—if naive—resolution: Shadbolt, *Emily Carr*, 90.

12 The hundreds of drawings: *Ibid.*

12 With characteristic determination: Carr, *Growing Pains*, 429.

12 The "new art": Shadbolt, *Emily Carr*, 30.

13 His work is distinguished by: Ian M. Thom, *Emily Carr in France* (Vancouver: Vancouver Art Gallery, 1991), 14.

13 She had an aversion: Blanchard, *The Life of Emily Carr*, 11.

14 Although there was: Carr, *Growing Pains*, 437. See also Carr's 1927 autobiographical note, sent to the National Gallery, quoted in Tippett, *Emily Carr: A Biography*, 142.

14 In an impassioned reply: *Vancouver Province*, Vancouver, 8 April 1912, 5, quoted in Tippett, *Emily Carr: A Biography*, 101.

15 A conflict is evident: Doris Shadbolt, *The Art of Emily Carr* (Toronto: Clarke, Irwin; Vancouver: Douglas & McIntyre, 1979), 38.

15 Carr spoke about native people: Blanchard, *The Life of Emily Carr*, 135; Shadbolt, *Emily Carr*, 104.

16 Certainly, she was battling: Blanchard, *The Life of Emily Carr*, 135.

16 She incorporated native designs: Carr, *Growing Pains*, 439.

16 She later wrote: *Ibid.*

17 In the early 1920s: Blanchard, *The Life of Emily Carr*, 168.

18 But she also understood: Shadbolt, *Emily Carr*, 41.

18 Carr had read Housser's book: Shadbolt, *The Art of Emily Carr*, 53.

18 Through the Group's methods: Shadbolt, *Emily Carr*, 41.

18 After her first visit: Carr, *Hundreds and Thousands*, 656.

19 "I think perhaps": *Ibid.*, 658.

19 Carr, too, attempted: Shadbolt, *The Art of Emily Carr*, 56.

19 In the meantime: *Ibid.*, 58.

19 "Sketch-sack on shoulder": Carr, *Growing Pains*, 443.

20 As in her earlier paintings: Shadbolt, *Emily Carr*, 123.

20 Although Carr was striving: Tippett, *Emily Carr: A Biography*, 172.

20 It is a curious paradox: Shadbolt, *The Art of Emily Carr*, 72.

21 Other influences of the time: *Ibid.*, 59.

21 As Carr wrote: Carr, *Klee Wyck* in *The Emily Carr Omnibus*, ed. Doris Shadbolt (Vancouver/Toronto: Douglas & McIntyre: 1993), 49.

21 In her dark, formalist works: Tippett, *Emily Carr: A Biography*, 167.

22 In many paintings of this period: Shadbolt, *Emily Carr*, 85.

22 She was apparently responding: Shadbolt, *The Art of Emily Carr*, 76.

23 After 1931, Carr established a "pattern": Shadbolt, *Emily Carr*, 112.

23 In her journals: Emily Carr, unpublished Journals, n.d., quoted in Blanchard, *The Life of Emily Carr*, 229.

24 Carr had been a "compulsive" scribbler: Shadbolt, *Emily Carr*, 21; Blanchard, *The Life of Emily Carr*, 208.

25 *The Book of Small*, recollections: Blanchard, *The Life of Emily Carr*, 272.

26 Her journals of 1937: Carr, *Hundreds and Thousands*, 860.

45 Recent research by Doris Shadbolt suggests that the carved figure Emily Carr identified as Totem Mother may be a male figure—a mythical cannibal holding its child victim.

54 Again, readers should be aware that Emily Carr sometimes misread the native carvings she depicted in paint and print, perhaps because of misinformation provided her or perhaps out of her own need to identify herself with this powerful art. The figure she names here as D'Sonoqua (or Zunoqua) was probably male, an inside house post at Quattiche (or Quattische) in Quatsino Sound. See Shadbolt, *The Art of Emily Carr*, p. 205 and Blanchard, *The Life of Emily Carr*, p. 311.